What others are saying about "The Hat That Saved My Life."

"I tore through that book very quickly, riveted to every page. My sister has had cancer twice. This book told me many of the things I wanted to know, and also gave me added skills in how to help her, or any other cancer victims I meet, even through just small acts. I find it odd after being a police officer for 9 years, and being an Army Reservist who has been deployed to Iraq, that I'd have any trouble talking to people about rough topics. I guess this was a bridge I had yet to cross—this was my family... I want to thank you, Mrs. Olson for having the courage to share all these private experiences with the public. You've done a great service."

Shanona T. Gregozek, SSG, USA

"Your book has been making the rounds with my friends, family, my Mom and it is now on its way to Florida. It is truly a great read and very inspiring."

Julie, San Jose, CA

"Becky is a phenomenal public speaker and one of the most inspirational individuals I have ever met. I worked with Becky to publish her book, The Hat That Saved My Life, which chronicles her struggle and victory over breast cancer. Her courage, humor and enthusiastic approach to life are contagious."

Kristen Morris, V.P., Quality Code Publishing, Seattle, WA

"Recently I was diagnosed with Breast Cancer. Our oldest daughter brought me your book, "The Hat that Saved My Life" It's the only book I have read in years. Your book helped me in so many ways. It's a wonderful book and Thank You for writing it!!!!! I hope you're winning with "round 2". God Bless."

Nancy, Palmdale, CA

"One word times a million = AMAZING!!"

Heather, Portland, OR

"...heart warming and inspiring... I am proud to have it, and will be showing it to others. With all my good wishes"

Sally, London, England

"Becky has found her own voice after her cancer initiation. Her mission is to inspire, comfort and befriend. These are rare and precious gifts, and Becky gives them freely, and humbly. In her own voice — often laughing and often crying — Becky is making the lives of many people brighter. What more can you ask?"

Dr. Ken Weizer, Director of Integrative Medicine, Providence Cancer Centers, Portland, OR

"Thanks for your inspired work. Your book so beautifully demonstrates and narrates your learning and sharing . . . and your encouragement to heal and love those around us. That's why we are here!!!"

Grant Werschkull, Conservation Solutions, Sacramento, CA

"I loved it! I read it straight through — her voice is great, compelling and really drew me in. I can easily see readers responding to the book!"

Elizabeth Watzke, Ph.D., Marylhurst University, Lake Oswego, OR

• • •

What others are saying about Becky M. Olson as a speaker

"Thank you for all you do in the fight against breast cancer. I'm proud to know you!"

Christine McDonald, Executive Director, Susan G. Komen Breast Cancer Foundation, Oregon and S.W. Washington Affiliate

"Your talk was wonderful and you are very courageous women. It is people like you who can show the rest of us that cancer is just a word, and not a sentence."

Diana Keith, Oregon Mammography Directive, Portland, OR

"I was able to hear you speak in Lafayette, LA and I want to thank you for motivating me again! You see, I too believe that things happen for a reason and God puts people in our lives for a reason. I didn't realize how down I was until I heard you. I just want to say thank you from the bottom of my heart, and please don't ever stop doing what you're doing. You have a gift, and you touch more lives than you know!" God Bless You!

Louise, Lafayette, LA

"Becky Olson spoke at our Special Friends Celebration, September 24, 2005. She spoke to over 800 breast cancer survivors and supporters. Becky was very warm, entertaining and well received by our audience. She is highly referred by our organization and by me as well.

John J. Edney M.D., Aesthetic Surgical Images, Omaha NE

"Becky was vivacious, fun, interesting, and heartwarming. She won't disappoint you. She is a professional who knows how to speak to large groups. We had over 800 in attendance. The audience truly enjoyed her. Becky sent a videotape to us to help in making our decision, and I must say, it does not do her justice. Your audience will love her."

Mary Lynn Schwietz, Chairperson, Special Friends Celebration, Omaha, NE

Becky Olson's humor and spirit are infectious, even in the face of pain and suffering, and she displays both in abundance as she tells of her struggle against breast cancer. The effect puts everyone who hears her humor at ease. Her essential message – as told in her book "The Hat That Saved My Life" and through her inspirational speaking – is that the human spirit can be the greatest weapon ever created against life-threatening illness. It is greater than all the medicine, all the scientific advances ever developed. And if you lose that spirit, then the battle is all but over. Becky shows how her own spirit and zest for living sustains not just her, but those who hear her message. It provides hope for all who endure the fear that cancer brings. Becky provides living, breathing proof of the power of the human spirit. It, and she, are indomitable.

John Kanelis, Editorial Page Editor, Amarillo Globe News, Amarillo, TX

"Speaking from personal experience and from her heart, Becky Olson is a jewel of a cancer survivor. Her animated spirit, insight and wit helped her through her own breast cancer experiences, but by her sharing, she helps others through theirs. Choosing life was the only option for Becky, and her insight on how family members and friends can respond when cancer is in the home, will help family members and friends know what to do to help their loved ones choose life too. A joy, an inspiration and a witty, articulate speaker, Becky just makes any listener's heart grow warmer and head grow smarter."

Carol Farron, Lodi Memorial Hospital,
Community Development Director, Lodi, CA

"I urge everyone who has a chance to hear Becky speak, please do. She was able to include humor into an otherwise, very serious subject. It is something that would be beneficial not only to women of all ages, but also to male family members of women who have breast cancer. She came across very sincere and caring. After listening to Becky, I know that if cancer does happen to anyone in my circle of friends, it will be easier to face."

Alice Bernard, Treasurer FMCA, Red Hat Luncheon, Albany, OR

"You were such an inspiration to everyone that was there and everyone after that day who heard about your courage."

Valerie Fielder, Director of Marketing, St. Bernard's Medical Center, Jonesboro, AK

"You deserved the standing ovation. You're one brave, inspiring little woman!!!!!" (Komen Survivor Luncheon)

Rachel Clearwater, Author, Portland, OR

"It was wonderful to have you as our speaker (at our annual survivor luncheon). You were inspiring, thought provoking, entertaining and funny! I have reviewed the evaluations and they were very, very positive. (Including: Becky Olson was a 5+++, -out of 5- , Becky showed remarkable courage, Becky was GREAT, Becky Olson was inspiring, Becky was sweet and gracious and she had great points). For me, you embodied our luncheon theme, "Thriving after Breast Cancer." Thank you!!!"

Heather Hill D.M.D., Susan G. Komen Board Member and Luncheon Committee Co-Chair, Oregon & S.W. Washington Affiliate

"It was beautiful, warm, witty and from the heart. I really enjoyed you! Your attitude is exuberant and contagious!"

Marcia, Pink Ribbon Survivor Celebration, Merryville, IN

"One of the best presentations we've ever had!"

Ruth Melvin, Marketing Director, St. John's Hospital, Longview, WA

The Hat That Saved My Life

A Story About Surviving Breast Cancer

Becky M. Olson

CLASSIC DAY PUBLISHING

Seattle, Washington
Portland, Oregon
Denver, Colorado
Vancouver, B.C.
Scottsdale, Arizona
Minneapolis, Minnesota

First Printing, August 2004
Second Printing, January 2007

ISBN: 1-59849-028-1
Library of Congress Control Number: 2006936045

Printed in the United States of America

Copies of this book can be purchased on-line at:
www.beckyolson.com

Design: Soundview Design Studio
Becky M. Olson Logo Design: WAE Technologies, Inc.
Editors: Don Roff, Gary Strait and Beth Watzke

CLASSIC DAY PUBLISHING

Classic Day Publishing
2925 Fairview Avenue East
Seattle, Washington 98102
877-728-8837
info@peanutbutterpublishing.com

Foreword

When my mama asked me to write a foreword for her book, I felt a rush of pride. Knowing that this suggestion came from a place of love and friendship, I felt nothing but honor. It wasn't but three seconds later, however, that I felt nothing but panic!

How could I even begin to write something worthy of this request? How do I accurately and vividly introduce this labor of love? How do I justify my pride, love, and friendship with this incredible woman?

Well, I learned my lesson the hard way once before. A side note for all you sappy daughters out there: don't write cheesy poems when you are 15-years-old about your mom's battle with breast cancer. There's no telling if she's going to write a book eight years later and publish the darn thing! (Skip to page 46 for a quick visit to the cheese factory.)

And so, I've placed a bit of pressure on myself this time around. I don't have my sophomore English teacher to lay down the rules of writing poetry that I can later blame for my overly-dramatized alliterations. I simply have my heart and rusty writing skills to guide me. I want to write something that will stand the test of time; that will make my mama proud, make her laugh, smile, and maybe even cry.

So here it goes…

When people tell me I look like my mom, the conversation generally goes like this: "You look so much like your mom." And mom says, "Yeah, maybe when I was 30 years younger and five kids thinner!" And I chime in with "Oh, mama, I'll catch up in five kids too."

What my mother doesn't know is that I beam inside when people—especially those close to mom—offer this observation. I like to think that they see the resemblance in not only our prominent apple-shaped cheek bones, our olive complexions, our chestnut hair, our dark wiry eyebrows, and the faint dark circles that frame our almond shaped eyes. I would like to think that it's the warmth of our touch when we're first introduced, the sound of our laughter or spark of life in our eyes. I would like to think it's my mother's spirit they see in me that compels them to say, "You look so much like your mother."

My fear is that when my mom hears this statement, she is instantly sent back in time and sees, for a brief moment, herself at 23-years-old. I see her checking herself up and down, and comparing her now scarred body, or her increase in dress size. She thinks of her career changes from the "indie" city life to that of corporate suburbia. These comparisons result in her dismissive comment, and what I fear most is that she doesn't truly know that people who know my mother see a light that reminds you of the early morning sun creeping onto your bedroom pillow; they hear a giggle that challenges that of a child;

they feel the warmth and softness of a wise old man; if they're as lucky as me, they smell the sweetness of a working mother.

If you are ever lucky enough to meet my mom, you will go into sensory overload in the best of ways. If you are ever fortunate enough to be friends with my mom, you will have one of the best gifts of your life.

And if she ever introduces us, I just hope that you feel compelled to say, "You look so much like your mom."

I speak for my entire family when we say—thank you for reading this book and becoming a part of our life!

Elizabeth Olson

Becky, Bill and all the kids at home, Christmas 2001. Top row: JoAnn, Joshua, Becky, Tanya, Beth. Bottom row: Micah, Elijah, Bill.

Preface

This book was written with love and tremendous respect for breast cancer patients—as well as their caregivers—whether they be friends or family members. We are all in this together!

• • •

We will all be touched by breast cancer in some way. It is estimated that nearly one in eight women will be diagnosed with the disease sometime in her life. The other seven will know her.

Some of us will lose someone we love.

Does someone you love have breast cancer? Perhaps it is a family member or close friend. Maybe it is someone you care about, but are less intimate with like a neighbor or co-worker.

As the caregiver, hopefully you will find my story helpful in giving you an understanding of what it feels like to go through a cancer diagnosis and treatment. Perhaps through my story, you will relate to the fear, the loneliness and the isolation that the patient often experiences.

Perhaps you will learn as I did the importance of humor and the impact that it had on my survival.

I will share with you some of the wonderful and practical things that others did for me. My hope is that should you have a loved one or close acquaintance who has been diagnosed with breast cancer, you can understand what she is experiencing and use the ideas in my book to help her survive.

Some of these ideas take only a few minutes but the thoughtfulness will be remembered for a lifetime. Help her. She will feel better and so will you.

• • •

If you are the one that is facing treatment for breast cancer, please know that you are among greatness. Over 200,000 women will be diagnosed in the United States this year. That's over 500 per day.

The survival rate is improving. You are in a sisterhood that only we can understand. Once a member, we will be connected forever. You are beginning a journey that will take you to places you've never been before. I've met some amazing people on my journey. You will meet them too.

As a sister survivor, perhaps this book will give you hope that the best is yet to come.

Dedication

This book is dedicated to:

My husband, Bill, for his strength, courage and unwillingness to give up.

My children, Micah, Elijah, Beth, Joshua, and Tanya for their unbelievable wisdom and love.

Patty and Dennis Winningstad who provided inspiration (and the hat) for this book.

Sharon Henifin, my dear friend and co-founder of Breast Friends, for her amazing support.

Heather O'Shaughnessy, a friend and co-worker who helped me look forward to each day.

• • •

I would also like to honor my professional team and clients:

Madalene Anderson, the nurse practitioner who discovered the lump. Without her I may not have survived to tell this story.

What others are saying about "The Hat That Saved My Life."

"I tore through that book very quickly, riveted to every page. My sister has had cancer twice. This book told me many of the things I wanted to know, and also gave me added skills in how to help her, or any other cancer victims I meet, even through just small acts. I find it odd after being a police officer for 9 years, and being an Army Reservist who has been deployed to Iraq, that I'd have any trouble talking to people about rough topics. I guess this was a bridge I had yet to cross—this was my family... I want to thank you, Mrs. Olson for having the courage to share all these private experiences with the public. You've done a great service."

Shanona T. Gregozek, SSG, USA

"Your book has been making the rounds with my friends, family, my Mom and it is now on its way to Florida. It is truly a great read and very inspiring."

Julie, San Jose, CA

"Becky is a phenomenal public speaker and one of the most inspirational individuals I have ever met. I worked with Becky to publish her book, The Hat That Saved My Life, which chronicles her struggle and victory over breast cancer. Her courage, humor and enthusiastic approach to life are contagious."

Kristen Morris, V.P., Quality Code Publishing, Seattle, WA

"Recently I was diagnosed with Breast Cancer. Our oldest daughter brought me your book, "The Hat that Saved My Life" It's the only book I have read in years. Your book helped me in so many ways. It's a wonderful book and Thank You for writing it!!!!! I hope you're winning with "round 2". God Bless."

Nancy, Palmdale, CA

"One word times a million = AMAZING!!"

Heather, Portland, OR

"...heart warming and inspiring... I am proud to have it, and will be showing it to others. With all my good wishes"

Sally, London, England

Table of Contents

Prologue

In 1996, I lived through the greatest challenge of my life. It was a time that I hope never to repeat. Looking back, however, I have discovered that I wouldn't trade that time or experience for anything.

I learned some things that forever changed my life. I've been blessed with new friendships that I never would have made. I changed my priorities at work, which unfortunately, seemed that I valued more than my own family.

I learned the importance of unwrapping my "gift," something you will hear about in a later chapter.

• • •

Looking back on my life, there is one word that describes me best.

Fighter!

At age sixteen, I worked at a fast food restaurant in Seattle, Washington. It was my first job. I worked hard and made good tips delivering food to dine-in-your-car customers. I didn't really like my job, but it paid for trips to the mall with my friends.

I tolerated my job. However, my boss was another matter. I didn't like him at all.

I always arrived at work early so I could get my company vest and hat on in time to start my day. One day I arrived early as usual and was in the back room getting ready for my shift. I had just buttoned up the orange and white striped vest and secured the matching hat with a bobby pin. I was bending over to tie my shoe when my boss sneaked up behind me and pinched my butt. "We need to add a little meat to those bones," he said.

"Oh, yeah?" I responded. "I quit."

With no additional comment, I threw the hat on the floor, ripped off the vest and threw it at the owner's fat head. I went next door, called my mom and she came to pick me up.

By age eighteen I decided that I knew more than my parents. I knew everything!

Armed with my high school diploma, I entered business school, and less than one year later I met a thirty-one year old man who would soon be my first husband. I quit school and got a job—and against my father's wishes—we got married a few months later.

Two years later I got pregnant, and two kids later, got divorced.

At age 26, single again, and a lot smarter, I took a weekend trip by boat from Seattle to Victoria, B.C., Canada. It was July, 1979. I went with a man I'll call "Dick," in an attempt to get to know him a little better. Within an hour of being together on the boat, we knew we had nothing in common. We finished the trip together, but again, the fighter in me knew this was the most it would ever be. We hardly spoke.

The trip back to Seattle was beautiful, however. The weather was gorgeous. The sky was bright blue, not a cloud overhead. It seemed that everyone on the boat was crammed into a small area on the back deck to enjoy the sunshine for the four hour trek back to Seattle. It looked like standing room only as Dick and I tried to join the crowd.

Within moments of stepping foot on board, we realized there would be no place for us in the back and we were doomed to the humid interior of the ship. However, just as we were turning to make our way toward the door into the ship's dark and dreary cabin, I saw him.

Across the crowded back deck of the ship, I caught a glimpse of a young handsome man. He appeared to be waving at us. As I focused on him, I realized he was yelling something at us. Intrigued, I listened more intently and realized he was telling us that he had two seats near him and we were welcome to join his group. I smiled at Dick and told him, "Hey we don't have to go inside. There's room over there." I pointed at that handsome man.

Dick frowned.

We made our way toward the two empty chairs, which by now were the envy of all the people standing nearby. My eyes, however, were on the young man. He was slender, tan, blue-eyed with dark hair. He was dressed in all white, white slacks, white shirt, just like the good guy in a movie. Our eyes met and a spark flew between us, and we were still twenty feet away from each other.

We got closer and the sparks intensified. I knew there was something special about this man. When we finally stood face to face, he told me his name was "Bill." Suddenly, I wished I had left Dick in Canada.

Conversation came easily between us and we were careful to include my travel partner. I could tell that Bill wasn't sure about the relationship between me and the man I boarded the boat with. I was eager to tell him but I didn't want to be rude.

As the trip progressed, we became better acquainted. Stolen moments here and there gave way to private conversations. Eventually, Bill found out that Dick and I lived in Seattle.

When it was getting close to departure time, Bill asked if the three of us could exchange addresses and phone numbers. We did. He very discreetly checked the addresses and phone numbers we both provided and realizing they were not the same, crumpled one into a little ball and placed the other in his pocket. I saw the action and we smiled at each other.

Leaving the boat a short time later was difficult. I knew I would never see Dick again. That didn't bother me. What did bother me was that I wasn't sure I would ever see this handsome young man again. Our clandestine conversations in the snack line were the best moments of the trip and I didn't want it to end.

It did, and we parted ways at the exit ramp.

Eventually Bill and I re-connected and scheduled another time to get together.

Over the next few months, we met regularly. He would come to Seattle or I would go to Portland. Being a single mom was difficult, but I was a fighter and I knew that I was better off raising my children alone than staying married to my first husband. Having Bill in my life was helpful. He fell in love with my two children and we fell in love with each other.

• • •

In April of 1980, at age 27, I placed my home for sale in Seattle and moved my children to Portland. Bill and I were married one month later, on May 17, the day before Mt. St. Helens erupted. (Our friends often joke about the hidden meaning behind the event on the mountain.) The four of us began our life together.

We got pregnant one month after our wedding, and when I was six months into my pregnancy, Bill was offered a job in Medford, Oregon.

We moved less than 30 days later. We discovered the home of our dreams. It was a drafty, old, yet beautiful home. It was built in 1935. The home had in-laid hardwood floors, high ceilings and French doors. It had been vacant for a year, so the price was right. It was tricky figuring out how to pay for it because my house in Seattle hadn't even had a nibble. We said a prayer over lunch and to our surprise discovered that God must have been holding it on the market just for us because my house in Seattle sold the same day.

The sale was clean and easy and we were able to move in within days of finding it. Everything was going great. I would stay home and enjoy my pregnancy and remain home with my new baby. However, the first month's heat bill sent me in search of a new job.

Being a fighter, I couldn't believe that no one would hire me just because I was eight months pregnant. Totally distressed by our financial situation, I found I really only had one option. I became a Tupperware lady.

I met some neighbors, booked some parties and stayed busy up until the day that Beth was born.

After her birth, I took a few weeks off but the bills kept coming in and we didn't have enough money to meet our monthly expenses. I decided to return to work. I had held jobs since I was sixteen years old with that first job at the fast food restaurant.

No longer pregnant, I knew I could get a real job. I liked selling plastic bowls but I figured out right away that the way to make money in Tupperware was to become a manager. It was hard work, but being a fighter, I figured out exactly what I needed to do and began systematically working through the objectives. I became a manager four weeks later.

The company car was a great addition to the family.

I continued to thrive in the business. I was so dedicated to my success that even pregnancy wouldn't stop me.

We became pregnant with our second child, Elijah. I worked throughout that pregnancy too, holding parties, managing a team of about twenty dealers, attending conferences and seminars.

One particular day, when our son was ten days away from his due date, I held three parties, one in the morning, one in the afternoon, and one later that evening. I was completely exhausted from packing and unpacking bags and hauling things in and out of my car. My back hurt, my feet ached and I was running on fumes, but too tired to eat.

I remember feeling particularly irritable and told Bill that night as we crawled into bed, "If I don't have this kid tonight, I'm not having him." I went into labor six hours later. Fighter!

• • •

I enjoyed selling Tupperware because it gave me the opportunity to be home when the kids needed me.

Somewhere in there, I had our third child, (my fifth), Micah.

However, due to some unfortunate circumstances, my husband lost his job. The economy was tough and he had a difficult time finding another one, so I decided to give up Tupperware and move onto some other opportunities. I knew it would be hard being away from the kids all day. But, we had five kids and no steady source of income.

I found a full-time job as the Director of Advertising for the Chamber of Commerce in Medford. I worked really hard and we more than doubled our advertising revenues the first year.

I continued to work hard and finally made the move to Corporate America. I had a chance to work for the largest yellow pages company in the northwest. I knew there was big money in that industry, but the hours would be grueling. I was up to the challenge and took a job in the Medford office.

Things were moving along nicely. Work was challenging and I was quite successful. We found great daycare for the kids. Life at home was good, so I thought. I knew we'd been through some difficult times, but we were no different than most families. Overall, it seemed that we were doing well. Sadly, I wouldn't have noticed otherwise. I was too busy.

Less than a year later, I had the chance for a promotion but it meant a move to Portland, Oregon, nearly six hours away by car. We put the house on the market, but this time, we waited.

Accepting the promotion, I traveled the 275 miles to Portland on Sunday and returned home the following Friday. Bill stayed in Medford with the kids, hoping the house would sell. I stayed with Bill's mom in Portland during the week, hoping for the same.

This went on every week for the next thirteen months.

Every Sunday, the kids cried as I was ready to leave, "Mommy, don't go."

Every Sunday, I cried as I drove away.

I didn't realize how difficult this was for my husband. He was job-hunting, while taking care of the house, the family, and waiting for someone—anyone—to make us an offer.

We continued living in this nightmare for over a year. The real estate market had taken a turn for the worse. We couldn't sell the house, so we decided that enough was enough and we took out a second mortgage on our Medford home. We used the extra money to make a down payment on a house in Portland.

Soon after, we moved the family to our new home and then placed our Medford home on the rental market.

I didn't miss a beat. Working twelve to fourteen hour days, and living together in the same house once again, I still didn't see my family. I was winning awards and receiving recognition. I believed it was okay because it meant more money for my family.

This went on for the next four years.

• • •

Finally, in 1996, at age 43, I was given news that stopped me cold.

I was told, "You have breast cancer."

Bill and Becky at her company sales award trip in New York City – 1993. "This photo is my constant reminder that our lives can change in an instant."

PART 1

The Hat That Saved My Life

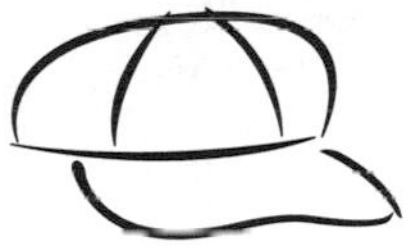

CHAPTER 1

The Discovery

Sharon turned off the ignition and we sat together in silence. The gloom of the hospital garage closed in around me. Squealing tires echoed against the cold, gray walls as someone made the turn toward the exit. Lucky for them, they were leaving this horrible place.

I was afraid to move. In my mind, I was sitting on the edge of a very high cliff. One move in the wrong direction would plunge me to my death. Somehow if I just stayed planted to the seat, the rest of this would go away. On this day, my life changed forever. On this day, I understood my own mortality.

And on this day, I asked God, "Why me?"

• • •

It started on Wednesday, April 24, 1996, on my way to the appointment, the necessary evil that my doctor had insisted I attend. I was in a hurry. I made the appointment for 7:30 a.m. so I could make my 9:00 a.m. sales call to see the most important client in my portfolio. I had absolutely no time for things like this.

Dressing for the day in everything appropriate for a sales call, I put on everything but my deodorant. The receptionist told me not to wear deodorant because it would interfere with the procedure. I figured a quick smashing of the breast, a smattering of deodorant, throw my shirt and jacket back on and I'd be on my way.

On this day in April, the day I was too busy for the mammogram, I dressed in my best wool-knit, navy blue pantsuit. I wore the blue, white and gold earrings my 15-year old daughter had given to me on a birthday years before. Beth was my fashion goddess. In her early childhood she had a knack for picking outfits that her friends admired—even before the fashion magazines declared them acceptable. My shoulder length, dark hair was pulled back into a low ponytail and held in place with a navy blue ribbon.

I worked late the night before to prepare myself for my sales appointment. My briefcase was loaded with the information I needed for my customer. I was ready. I just needed to get this stupid mammogram out of the way.

Fighting my way through rush hour traffic and heavy rain, I cursed the nurse practitioner for forcing me to schedule this appointment.

I arrived for my mammogram just before 7:30 a.m. Always on time: that was my motto. Three other women were in the waiting room when I arrived. "Oh great," I thought to myself. "I hurried, now I get to wait."

Sitting impatiently in the waiting room, I checked my

watch as I mindlessly flipped through magazines. I waited for someone—anyone—to call my name. They didn't.

My mind shifted to work. Deep in thought about my upcoming sales call, I rehearsed my opening remarks over and over again. You can never be too prepared: my second motto. I was just coming in for the kill when I was startled back to reality. Finally, I heard my name.

If you are under 40, you've likely never had a mammogram. There are two things you should know, besides no deodorant. First, the technician will escort you to the dressing room where you strip from the waist up and put on one of those goofy blue hospital gowns that open in the front. And second, you wait.

I went into my own private little dressing room, stripped as instructed and checked my watch. The technician eventually returned and the two of us proceeded to the mammography room.

We entered the dimmed room. "How nice, mood lighting," I thought. The large metal machine hummed and welcomed me like a giant mechanical vise, its arms outstretched as if waiting for a hug.

The technician shut the door. She told me to stand in front of the machine and open my gown. She lifted and pushed parts of my breasts I never knew I had. She positioned my breast "just so" on the machine platform.

And then came the torture.

She hit the button on the machine and the platforms began to close in on each other. The only thing stopping them from resting firmly against each other was my breast.

I was certain the machine would stop its approach any second, but it kept moving. My full breast was suddenly squished as flat as a Frisbee between the platforms. I thought it had been flattened clear into the next room.

"Hold your breath and don't move," she said as she stepped behind the Plexiglas barrier.

Taking in a final shallow breath through my nose, I held very still. "Heaven forbid I should move and have to do this again," I thought.

The big machine vibrated for a second and I imagined I could hear the sounds of the camera lenses clicking as they created the X-ray. She positioned me several different ways and we repeated the process.

Finally, she got all the different angles she needed and I was free to leave this torture chamber. She sent me back to the curtained off dressing room. Another wait.

Sitting in that little room, I flipped through the same magazine.

Under normal circumstances, if all goes well, the technician will be back shortly and say, "It looks good, go ahead and get dressed."

When she came back and pulled open the curtain, I fully expected to hear the desired message. Instead, I saw a look on her face that told me a different message was about to be delivered.

"The doctor would like some more pictures. Please follow me," she said coldly.

I put the magazine down, grabbed the front of my gown to hold it shut and followed her back into that room with the hideous machine. I kept thinking all the way, "I'm sure it's nothing. She probably just messed up."

We went through the same procedure, and again I went to my little room and waited. By now, I was pretty annoyed—not to mention a little sore.

I really didn't have time to wait for her to get it right. It was close to 9:00 a.m. and calling my customer to tell him I was running late was out of the question. My cell phone wouldn't work in the room, probably due to interference from all the equipment. So I waited. Again.

I was sure the second set would result in the message I wanted to hear the first time, that everything was fine. This was not the case. She came back a third time and finally a fourth. On the fourth visit to my holding cell, I was told that I had graduated to the ultrasound machine. Now, I was starting to get scared. What I thought was an error on her part was turning into something much worse.

I'd had ultrasounds several times before during my pregnancies. The fact that doctors could tell that the black and white tissue on the monitor was a baby was both encouraging and exciting.

I wasn't sure what the doctor wanted to look at on the monitor this time, but I was quite sure it wasn't a baby.

I entered the ultrasound room, and this time instead of standing in front of a machine that would squish my breasts, I was asked to lie down on the gurney. The radiologist put some warm gel on my breast, just like they did on my stomach so many times before. He gently slid the wand back and forth over my breast and finally settled on one spot.

A few seconds brought clarity to the screen as he continued to look at the monitor.

I didn't like the expression on his face.

Slowly turning my gaze from his face to the screen, my eyes focused on random blobs on the monitor. With much difficulty, I finally saw the monster that the radiologist had been looking at.

I suddenly felt transported into a Hollywood movie. I hadn't seen "Alien" in quite a long time, but I thought I was about to give birth to one. The ultrasound revealed a mass of tissue with tentacles that seemed to reach into my soul. I thought I was looking at some kind of animal. The body was shaped like a sea horse, curved from top to bottom, but it had claws like a scorpion.

My head began to spin and I could barely breathe.

The next words from the radiologist were words I never dreamed of hearing. "I can't be 100% positive, but I think you have breast cancer."

He went on to tell me how sorry he was and urged me to make an appointment with a specialist as soon as possible for confirmation. He said he wished he had better news. Me too!

I went out to my car, in shock, in tears and madder than Hell. "How can this happen to me?" Cancer happens to other people, and old people. I was only 43, successful and busy.

I tried to call my husband on my cell phone, but I could not see the numbers through my tears.

After several attempts to dial, I finally got it right. My husband Bill answered the phone. Upon hearing his voice, I suddenly fell apart and cried out loud. He tried to console me, but he hadn't a clue as to what was happening. He knew I was upset, more so than he had witnessed in a long time.

He was sure I had lost my job. He knew how much I loved my job, and knew that anything other than losing it could not possibly cause such an emotional outburst. I don't remember much, but I do know that I told him that I wish it were that simple. That's when he knew it was something really bad.

I told him the mammogram revealed probable breast cancer and I needed to see a specialist. I couldn't believe these words were coming out of my mouth. Though I was not an exercise queen or nutritional guru, I led a fairly active life. I wasn't really overweight, I was just under height. In my mind, I was a thin person trapped in this robust body. Thin yet robust, active people don't get breast cancer.

After the call to my husband, I called my office and asked one of my co-workers to cancel my appointments. I asked her to call several of my customers and tell them that I had a family emergency and that I would reschedule later when I returned to work.

When I got home from my mammogram appointment, still wearing no deodorant, I suddenly didn't care. The sales call I missed no longer mattered.

I walked into my house, which was dirty and dusty from a major remodel that seemed never to end. The contractor had pulled the roof off the garage that morning and was gearing up to add the 500 sq. foot addition. "Funny," I thought, "my house is getting a nice upgrade while I'm falling completely apart."

I tried to ignore the construction workers, but it was pretty tough when they were walking in and out to use the bathroom.

I made my way to the kitchen, grabbed the phone book, and looked up my doctor's phone number. Shaking, I dialed the phone. The radiologist had already called the doctor, so he was expecting my call. He gave me a referral to a specialist.

I called the specialist for an appointment. The receptionist answered the phone, "Surgical Oncologists." I didn't like the sound of that. It sounded scary and quite official. I told her I needed to see someone right away. She told me their first opening was in two weeks.

"You don't understand. I don't wait well," I said. "I need to get in now."

She reconsidered and suddenly found an opening "tomorrow."

Distraught and confused, my solution was to open a bottle of wine I don't actually remember drinking it, but later, when our neighbor came over to talk to my husband about a trip the two had planned for the weekend, he saw the bottle of wine, half gone, and the X-rays lying on the counter.

"Bad news?" he asked.

"I believe so," I responded and poured myself another glass.

• • •

Slightly hung-over, I woke up the next morning, got cleaned up and left for the doctor's office. I didn't know what was going to happen and unlike my usual rush, I was in no hurry to find out.

My husband and I made the twenty minute drive to the clinic in total silence. He probably had the radio on, but I was oblivious to everything around me.

We finally arrived and I checked in with the receptionist. Sitting, waiting for the doctor, patiently this time, the nurse finally called me back to the examining room. My eyes became watery. I cried softly as I walked behind her.

Again, I stripped from the waist up and waited for the doctor to come in. I had not met him before. Changing doctors is difficult even in the best of times.

During my many pregnancies, I had changed doctors three times due to relocation, and once again because my doctor retired just as I became pregnant with my fifth child. This was not the best of times. In fact, it couldn't be much worse. The doctor I had become comfortable with was not here. The nurse practitioner that had so firmly persuaded me to have the mammogram was not here. This would be someone completely new to me.

When he finally walked in a few minutes later, I broke into tears. I don't remember him being particularly sympathetic. Without hesitation, he started talking about a needle biopsy. I didn't know what it was but I knew anything involving a needle couldn't be good. I decided that he must do this procedure frequently as a few tears from a hysterical woman didn't seem to soften him.

I reclined on the gurney and he swabbed my right breast with bright orange antiseptic ointment and without much conversation, pulled a large needle out of its wrapper. He explained that he was attempting to deaden the area so I wouldn't feel the next step.

A few minutes later he pulled an even larger needle from its wrapper, and inserted it into my breast where the other needle had been. With this step, he began the biopsy. He put the needle into the center of the mass and withdrew fluid and tissue from the lump. As the needle entered, he felt my body tense. He told me to relax. I remember thinking, "Hey buddy, let me stab you with a sharp metal object and see if you can relax." I was hopeful that his attempt to deaden the area had worked. It did. I felt very little pain, but my fear increased by the second.

As the needle remained in my breast, I tried to think of other things. I imagined my life as it was just a few days before. I thought about the people I would miss and wondered if they would miss me. I wondered if anyone would attend my funeral.

Finally free to get dressed, I made my way to the receptionist's desk and asked her what would happen next. She told me the tissue and fluid sample would be sent to a pathology lab for diagnosis.

I asked her, "When will you know the results?"

"Hopefully the results will be back tomorrow," she responded.

This was good news because that meant I wouldn't have to wait through the weekend to find out that this was only a horrible dream.

Friday morning finally came after a long and sleepless

night. I called the doctor's office several times that day to see if the report was back. The entire day came and went with no results. I was extremely distraught by the end of the day. I don't like loose ends and this one was going to ruin my weekend.

I knew that soon I would be alone. The event my husband had planned for that weekend with the neighbor was to go to "Promise Keepers" in Seattle. "Promise Keepers" is a Christian-based convention for men only. It would be held at the King Dome. Its purpose is to gather men together to bring them close to God, to pray for their families and receive guidance in their role as husband and father. There is some controversy around the fairness, the male only aspect, of the group, but I had no problem with it at all. He offered to stay home with me, but I selfishly told him no. I wanted him to go. After all, where else could he go to be with 65,000 men, all of them praying for their families. I knew I'd get a mega-dose of prayer if he went.

Our neighbor arrived at the house later that day. Bill was packed and ready to go when he arrived. I remember the look on Bill's face as he was getting ready to leave.

"Are you sure you want me to go, because I'll stay if you want," Bill said.

"Of course I want you to go. You've been planning this for sometime. Besides, I need your prayers," I was quick to respond.

CHAPTER 2

Alone

That evening, with the house empty, the loneliness began to settle in. My husband was in Seattle. My kids were at their friends' houses. I had not told them anything yet. Walking upstairs to my bedroom, I put on the only clothing that brought me comfort, my red and blue plaid flannel pajamas.

I considered going to bed but I knew I wouldn't sleep. My mind would soon be filled with all the "what ifs" the minute I set my head against the pillow. I decided instead to go back down stairs and watch television.

I wandered into the empty family room, grabbed a blanket off the back of the sofa, the remote control off the table next to my husband's favorite spot and curled up on the couch. I flipped the stations repeatedly, looking for something—anything—to replace the thoughts in my head. Nothing that night would be able to enter in and clear away the feeling of loneliness.

I thought about turning off the television and setting down the remote but my arms and hands could not respond. I've heard of people having near death experiences, but I thought that you had to be nearly dead for that to happen. Nevertheless, I was having one now. I knew that my body was still physically intact, and sitting motionless on the sofa. But I wasn't in it. I couldn't feel my legs, my arms or my hands. I stared endlessly at the television. The sound was on, but I didn't hear anything on the airwaves.

Later, when the feeling came back to my limbs, I got off the couch and made my way slowly up the stairs to my bedroom. I slowly crawled into bed.

I lay in bed for the longest time, thinking about things that I so often took for granted. For the first time in my life, I wondered what would happen to my family if I weren't around anymore. I wondered if I'd live long enough to cook one more Thanksgiving dinner.

Thanksgiving had always been the one holiday in our family that no one argued about as to where they would go for dinner. Everyone came to my house. Every year, I cooked a giant turkey, as big as I could find. I'd do it all, yams with brown sugar, fresh homemade cranberry sauce, green beans, pumpkin pie and whipped cream, sometimes from scratch. I always let Bill peel the potatoes and mash them. It was his job. I never told him about the little pogies, the brown spots that dig into the potatoes, only visible when you peel them, that I would cut out when he was done. I wondered who would do it for him if I wasn't here. Dinner was not complete without my favorite stuffing recipe. Every year I added my grandfather's secret ingredients, pine nuts, to the dressing. Every year, it all but disappeared on the first night. Barely any stuffing left over.

Every Thanksgiving, I thought about Papou, my grandfather. I would remember when I was young, he would tell me I better do something or he'd take his belt to me. I also remember the smile in his eyes as he said it. He would never take a belt to anyone, especially his grandchildren. He was an old, cranky, Italian teddy bear. I missed him every Thanksgiving. I missed him a lot that night.

Who would feed my family on Thanksgiving, if I were no longer on this earth?

I wondered if I would live long enough to hang the kids' Christmas stockings one more time. Our kids were old enough to question the existence of Santa, but they were smart enough not to talk about it. They knew I believed and besides they liked waking up on Christmas morning to all the little surprises stuffed into their stockings.

I wondered if I'd see my five children, ages eleven to twenty-three, graduate from high school or see them get married and become parents. I began to miss grandchildren that hadn't even been imagined yet. After several hours of thinking, my brain hurt. My heart felt heavy, like a water balloon. It was pounding in my chest and felt like it was ready to explode.

Sometime later, unable to get the rest I so badly needed, I got out of bed and walked to the full-length mirror attached to my sliding closet door. That mirror always failed to capture the essence of who I really was. I've learned over the years, that if I sucked in my stomach and held myself just right in front of it, I could remove five pounds. If I held my head up just right, I could eliminate my double chin. So even though it was easily fooled, the mirror had always been my friend. Only a friend can love you in spite of your flaws and make you think you are beautiful at the same time. But after today, the mirror would no longer be my friend.

It would show me all the things I didn't want to see.

I stood in front of the mirror, lifted my shirt and tried to imagine myself with one breast. That was difficult. I was a pretty well endowed woman, one benefit of being "robust." I turned from side to side and no matter which angle I looked at, one breast would either be ugly or gone. No matter how I held myself or positioned my shoulders, I could not replace the breast that would be removed. I couldn't trick anyone into thinking that my breasts were ever going to be the same again. I hated the fact that this mirror would never again lie to me. Again, I cried and went back to bed. I must have finally drifted off to sleep because the rest of the night came and went without my knowledge.

• • •

After a very long, lonely and sad weekend, I honestly thought I would never hear or feel joy again. Then my children came home. When they entered the house, they brought all the noise and joy that only children can bring.

They had no idea yet of the changes we were all about to experience.

It was so difficult to look at their beautiful faces and try to respond to their questions.

"What's for dinner?" Beth would ask

"Where are my shoes?" asked Elijah

"I can't find my backpack," Micah said.

I was quite proud of the acting job I did. My success at putting on a happy face and pretending that nothing was wrong covered the ache in my gut and the break in my heart. I needed my husband. I longed to hug him. I could hug my kids, I often did, but for some reason I was worried that they'd pick up on something and ask the question I dreaded most, "Is everything OK?"

I knew I couldn't lie to them, so I tried to keep my distance.

Bill finally arrived home some time later. I was never so happy to see him. He walked in the door and wrapped his big, strong arms around me and pulled me close. He simply held me. Words were unnecessary.

Later that night, we talked for what seemed like hours. We discussed how we would tell our children. We decided that we would wait for a final diagnosis before telling them anything. I thought, "Why worry them if it's not serious." We only had to wait another day or two, so we decided we could wait.

We went to bed that night wondering what Monday would bring.

CHAPTER 3

The Diagnosis

After a very fitful night, Monday finally arrived. With the kids out the door for school and Bill at work, I was alone again, but this time it was a good thing. With no one around, I could finally leave my smiling face behind and just be me. I was allowed to simply feel what I was feeling without having to cover anything.

At 10:00 a.m., I called the doctor's office to see if the result of my biopsy was available. I nearly turned blue holding my breath while the nurse pulled my chart.

She came back to the phone and said, "Let me get Rosie for you."

I was certain that because she wouldn't tell me anything and passed me off to the nurse, the news was not good.

A couple of minutes later, Rosie came to the phone and said the test was back.

"I'm sorry," she said. "The result is inconclusive."

"Inconclusive?" I railed back at her. "What does that mean?"

What that meant was that after waiting an entire weekend, anxious, scared and incredibly sad, the tissue sample was not good enough to make a diagnosis. It also meant I had to do it all over again. However, this time, it wouldn't be a simple needle biopsy in the doctor's office. I knew that I would be going into the hospital for a tissue biopsy (removal of the lump) and that the tissue would be sent to the pathologist for another report, which meant another long wait.

I was heartsick. This meant holding off even longer to tell my children, and even longer to know if I would live.

As I said earlier, I don't wait well, so we scheduled the biopsy for later that same week.

My first doctor, the one who did the needle biopsy, was not available, so they scheduled me with yet another doctor. The surgery would be in two days. I can handle two days, I thought.

I don't remember much about the next two days, but finally, the big day came. I got dressed and Bill drove me to the hospital. I told Bill that I would try not to think too much about it. It seemed that I often made mountains out of molehills and this was, after all, just another molehill. I would simply get this over with and not dwell on something that would probably turn out to be okay anyway.

My lips were moving as the words came out of my mouth, but my heart did not believe it.

We drove to the hospital in total silence, with me trying not to think about it—an impossible task.

My thoughts were dark. The questions of death rolled

around in my head, "What if I don't make it? Am I right with God? Will my husband find a new love interest? If so, how long will he wait? Will she look like me or be completely opposite? Will she love my children? Will they love her back? Will I be missed?"

Arriving at the hospital, feeling bona-fide crazy by then, we parked near the entrance. Still, without much conversation, I opened the car door and slid out. Bill and I walked arm in arm through the front door of the hospital. But I was mad at him for replacing me so quickly.

The receptionist checked me in, placed the little plastic bracelet on my wrist and called for an escort to the surgical ward. I undressed and put on the same type of goofy-looking gown I wore during the mammogram.

The surgical nurse came into the room to check on me. She spent the next few minutes prepping me, poking me and finally she asked me if I needed anything before they knocked me out. I told her I wanted to meet my doctor. We were new to each other and I wanted to see him. But more importantly, I wanted him to know the person he was about to slice open. I didn't want to be just a diseased breast to him.

I also wanted to confirm that he knew which side to cut into.

Earlier, I had considered making labels and attaching them to each boob, one that said "not this one" and the other would say "yes, but make it pretty." With all the anxiety of the day, I forgot to do it.

I waited on the gurney outside the operating room

silently praying when Dr. Wolf approached. I felt his presence even before I saw him. I opened my eyes and looked straight at him. His eyes were gently focused on me. He walked the last two feet towards me, tall, slender, with dark hair and sparkling blue eyes. He had a smile on his face easily detected under his green surgical mask.

I suddenly became very aware of the drab blue hospital gown that hid my body, and the makeup that remained in their bottles on my bathroom counter. I was embarrassed by my appearance, but when I saw the compassion in his bright blue eyes I knew I was in good hands.

He took hold of my hand and asked, "How are you feeling?"

"Scared," I said.

"I understand," he responded, "but we'll take very good care of you. I promise."

He held my hand the entire time we spoke. He told me that the next time I would see him would be when I woke up in the recovery room.

The hospital pastor came in next to say a prayer with me. A few moments later I was out cold.

I must have still been groggy on the drive home because I don't remember any of it.

• • •

I knew it would take a couple of days to get the report and for those two days life was surreal. I was somewhere between planning my future and planning my funeral.

I tried so hard to pretend nothing was wrong. If my kids needed something, I did my best to help them as I normally would, but a part of me was trying to teach them to do it themselves in case I wasn't around much longer. They learned how to do the laundry, how to make macaroni and cheese from a box, and how to get the recycling ready for Monday morning.

I probably scared the Hell out of them. My poor kids must have thought I was tired of raising them because it appeared I was getting them ready to move out on their own—and my oldest had just turned fifteen.

• • •

Finally the wait was over. Two days later I received the phone call I had been waiting for. They wanted to see me in person. I knew my life was about to change forever, one way or the other. Either I was cancer-free but had enough of a shock to change my life or I had cancer. They don't usually call you and make you come in to tell you the news is good, so I was quite certain it was the latter. I just didn't know how bad it was.

The image of the alien haunted me. Though it was no longer inside me, but was lying at the bottom of some scientist's petri dish, I wondered just how much damage it had done before they exorcised it.

I called my friend Sharon to tell her the report was in and I was heading to the doctor's office. Sharon was a breast cancer survivor and understood exactly what I was going through. She had gone through the same thing three years earlier.

"Do you want me to go with you?" Sharon asked.

"No," I said. "You're busy and I don't want you to feel like you have to go with me. I'm sure I can handle it alone."

"Don't be ridiculous," she said.

Sharon was the first among our circle of friends to be diagnosed with breast cancer. Sadly, I did to her what so many people do. I was there for her in the beginning, but eventually said to her, "Let me know if there is anything I can do for you." I meant it and then I went back to my busy life waiting for her to call.

She never did.

She spent much of her recovery alone. She was determined not to do the same to me.

I told her she didn't have to go with me, but inside I was screaming for support. Sharon knows me well. I was thrilled when she insisted that I let her come with me.

As the time grew closer to leave for my appointment, I changed out of my bathrobe, my new best friend, and pulled on my sweat pants and a T-shirt—a far cry from the navy blue pant suit I loved. Sharon arrived a few minutes later and we left in her car for the hospital.

I don't remember much about the ride. I do recall staring out the window, but the only thing I remember seeing were the raindrops clinging to the glass trying not to slide down the slippery surface. I became the rain, clinging to the glass, holding onto it as if my life depended on it. My world no longer existed outside that surface.

A storm was building and my world was closing in on me.

• • •

We finally arrived at the doctor's office. We pulled into the dark, gray cold parking structure and Sharon turned off the ignition. We sat quietly in the car. It seemed an eternity, yet Sharon honored my silence. She knew what was going on in my head. I am never silent. By nature I am chatty. I am also Italian and Greek, which explains why I talk with my hands. My hands weren't moving either. "Why me, God?" I asked silently.

After a few minutes of silence in the parking garage, I put my hand on the door handle, took a deep breath and we both opened our doors and got out. Sharon came around to my side and put her arm around me as we walked into the clinic.

The elevator ride to the ninth floor was the longest elevator ride I've ever taken. We stopped on every floor to let people off or to take on new passengers. For the first time in my life, the long ride was welcome.

Dr. Wolf's office was at the far end of the hall. As I stepped off the elevator and made the left turn to start the long walk, tears welled up in my eyes. Sharon saw them and hugged me tighter. Finally, after what seemed like the longest walk in history, we entered his office. Sharon escorted me to a chair and told me to have a seat while she checked me in.

A few minutes later, Bill arrived and took a seat by my

side. He looked worried. He had tears in his eyes. He put his strong, loving arms around me and held my head close to his chest. I lost it right then. I started sobbing. He pulled a hankie out of his sleeve just like he did on our wedding day. We waited for what seemed an eternity.

Finally, the nurse, Rosie, called my name and the three of us got up together. I didn't even have to ask if it was okay for them to accompany me. Rosie knew. She escorted all of us to a private waiting room just off the doctor's personal office. It was a pretty room, with pale pink walls, teal carpeting and a soft pastel sofa and matching chair. A floral centerpiece adorned the glass top table. On another day, this room might have provided me with the comfort it was designed for. Rosie said it would be a little while before the doctor would be in, but she wanted us to have some privacy.

"Rosie?" I asked, "Could you possibly give me some idea of what to expect?"

"I know you are anxious, but I really can't. The doctor will be in soon," she replied softly and closed the door quietly behind her.

We waited forever in that room. I became more and more anxious as the brief ray of sunshine that gleamed through the window, slowly disappeared.

The hankie was soaked. Bill handed me a box of Kleenex. I took several sheets and twisted them, tore them, and destroyed piece after piece. I made quite a pile.

I finally lost all composure and told Sharon I really needed to see the report. She and Bill tried to calm me but Sharon relented, got up out of her chair and slowly opened the door. Looking in both directions, she spotted Rosie. She left the room, briefly, closing the door behind her.

I don't know what Sharon said to her during her brief time in the hallway, but a few minutes later Rosie came into the room with a manila folder. She casually laid it on the table in front of me and left.

I stared at the file but I refused to touch it. It was as if the file itself had cancer, and touching it would somehow cause the cancer to rub off on me.

A couple of minutes later Sharon picked up the file and slowly opened it as if unwrapping a very fragile gift. She poured over the report and began to read portions to me.

As she read, a light blanket of fog was forming around me. She continued reading and the light fog became thick, dark, storm clouds. Everything tightened in around me.

Words like "aggressive" and "invasive" jumped off the page wrapping themselves around my brain like a python, squeezing as hard as it could. I held onto Bill's hand as hard as I could. His hand turned blue, but he didn't care.

I had nearly stage three breast cancer. This was not good. There are only four stages but unlike the Olympics, lower is better when it comes to a cancer diagnosis. I had lymph node involvement and there was cancer on the edge of the lump, which means when they removed the lump for the biopsy, they may have left some cancer cells behind. I knew I was going to die. I wondered again, if anyone would come to my funeral.

Just then, Dr. Blue Eyes came into the room. He saw my face and handed me another box of tissue. Sitting down on a chair facing me, he picked up the report that Sharon had replaced on the table. What he said next blew me back to reality.

"The bad news is you have breast cancer. The good news is you have garden variety breast cancer, meaning it is the most treatable and curable form we know of," he said.

He went on to tell me that although it was advanced, it was a good thing we found it when we did.

He kept talking, but all I heard were the magic words, "garden variety." I was sure that garden variety was a good thing.

"Does this mean that I can perhaps survive this?" I asked, rhetorically.

The cancer only invaded one lymph node out of the sixteen tested. I dread to think what would have happened had they checked only fifteen nodes and missed the one that was diseased. Perhaps they would have misdiagnosed me and not have taken it as seriously as they did. Even though the nasty little cancer cells had started to crawl through my body, none of them had found their way to any of my vital organs. At least not yet.

Suddenly, there was a tiny break in the storm clouds.

CHAPTER 4

The Decision

I had some big decisions to make. Fast! Unfortunately, fast is tough considering there are no easy answers when it comes to treatment options. Friends, God bless them, are filled with compassion and advice, but are sometimes as easily mislead as the patient. Every magazine and newspaper article spouts a different cure. Every television and supermarket tabloid would have you tromping all over the world in search of that cure. The Internet is loaded with intentions, but not all are good and many are not based on fact.

Every case is different, every cancer responds differently to treatment. If you have a friend that has had breast cancer, you can't expect that your treatment will be just like hers.

You also need the energy and presence of mind to deal with it. I remember very little about the next few days. I do, however, recall being torn between raging fear and total depression. Regardless of my emotional state, I didn't have time to sit back and wait for the right decision to come to me. I had to go find it.

I began my search for the answer with Sharon. She received her diagnosis three years earlier and had decided on mastectomy with reconstruction. I talked to her at length about what it was and how she felt it impacted her appearance. I asked her everything I could think of except, "Can I see it?"

When we seemed to come to the end of the conversation, she knew, because of the look on my face, that I still needed more information.

She asked, "Would you like to see it?"

"Can I really?" I asked without any hesitation.

We went up to my bedroom and I closed the curtains as she unbuttoned her blouse and unhooked her bra. I waited, somewhat embarrassed, but anxious. I'd never asked to see a woman's breasts before. I expected to see scars and unevenness. I expected to see a hideous monster.

To my surprise, everything looked normal and I could only see the tiniest of scarring along the surgical line. Her breasts were "perky" like a twenty-year-old. They looked better than mine had in years, and we were close to the same age. Yes indeed, mastectomy with reconstruction was one option that would make me look like Sharon. My cloud began to lift.

My second option was one I heard about many years before. A friend of mine with breast cancer had a surgical procedure called "Tram Flap." The doctor took fat, skin and muscle from her abdomen, and created a new breast.

Wow, imagine that! Getting a tummy tuck and new

breasts all at once, and even better yet, having it paid for by my insurance company. What a great concept.

The sun was shining and I was ready.

• • •

On the day of my follow-up appointment, I was ready and excited. I decided I would see my doctor and ask him about each of my two acceptable options and get his opinion. As I prepared for my appointment, I remember feeling a slight sense of relief. There were options after all, ones I could live with and I was ready to choose one of them.

The trip to the clinic was a lot more fun than the last time. I sang to the "Oldies" on the radio during the drive. This time there was a little more sunshine. Sunshine in Oregon is not guaranteed in the spring, but there was sunshine in my heart. I had already received the bad news. The rest was downhill and I felt it was time to get on with it. This time when I got to the parking garage, I quickly opened the door and couldn't wait to get to the doctor's office. In fact, I arrived early.

I was escorted by the receptionist to the same pretty room to begin my wait. I couldn't wait to see Dr. Blue Eyes. It wasn't long before he came in, or maybe it just seemed shorter, I really don't know.

Excitedly, I told him about the two options uncovered during my research. I was sure I was the first one to discover them. I couldn't wait to get his opinion on which of my two options I should consider. I would go along with his recommendation, I decided.

He smiled and then recommended something completely different. "Lumpectomy."

I had no idea what he was talking about, but I was determined not to let it ruin my mood. He went on to explain that recent research showed that lumpectomy, most of which had been done during the biopsy, followed by chemotherapy and radiation, was as effective in treating some cancers as mastectomy.

He believed it was a better option for me than the ones I had hoped for. He explained that I'd already had a partial lumpectomy during the earlier biopsy when the tumor had been removed along with extra surrounding tissue. However, according to the pathology report, there was evidence of cancer clear up to the edge of that tissue, which means there was still the probability of some cancer cells left behind in my breast.

If we decided to go that route, all we needed to remove was a little more surrounding tissue to complete the lumpectomy, then move on to chemotherapy and follow-up with radiation, or what I call L.C.R. For my particular situation, he felt that this procedure would be less invasive than a mastectomy, and with the chemotherapy and radiation, just as effective.

My vision of a flat tummy and perky breasts was fading fast. The clouds were rolling back in. This was a new option that I hadn't yet considered and I needed time to think about it. Though it was less invasive, it meant that I would have two very lopsided breasts. Also, he informed me that once radiation is performed on my affected breast, reconstruction may become more difficult because of the changes to the tissue caused by the radiation.

I felt like I was back where I started, confused, uncertain and now I had even more options to consider.

Armed with my doctor's recommendation, I boldly contacted my former physician in my old home town of Medford, Oregon, to get his opinion about L.C.R. It's not that I didn't trust my new doctor, but I wanted a second opinion. This was a big decision—life altering, in fact—and I wanted to make sure that both doctors agreed. I called his office in Medford. He was with a patient, so I asked for their fax number and faxed him the report. It wasn't long before he called back.

"Hi Becky, I just saw your report," he said. "It looks like you've been through the mill."

He sounded devastated. He had been our family physician for several years. We only changed doctors because we moved to Portland, Oregon. He was my age and this seemed to really hit him hard. I could hear his voice quiver as though he was on the verge of tears. We spoke for several minutes.

"I'm scared, but I'm all right," I said to reassure him.

After we got through our highly emotional conversation, he agreed that lumpectomy was a good option for me. I was disappointed. My vision of a new and improved version of me completely vanished.

It's funny how when we are faced with difficult choices,

we can make our decisions based on one thing. In reality, I could have gone with any decision I wanted. I could have chosen the more traumatic surgery and ended up with new, perky breasts. However, I quickly went into survival mode and chose survival over aesthetics.

I scheduled another surgery for the following week. This visit would have its own unique problems. I was there to have the rest of the tissue surrounding the lump removed. My doctor had warned me that finding the edges of the lump would be difficult. When he informed me that I had to go to the hospital early and have a wire inserted into the area where the tumor had been, I grew a little anxious. My face turned white as I envisioned thousands of hypodermic needles sticking out of my arm. I was snapped back to reality when he assured me it would only be one wire and that it was a necessary procedure. They had to know where to cut once they got inside. "Since the lump is gone, the task will be more difficult this time," he said.

Later that week, I was admitted to the hospital one more time. I had become a familiar face to the hospital staff by then and though I like it when, "everybody knows my name," as they say in "Cheers," I was tired of this drill.

The reason for this visit was that I have really bad veins. They tend to roll or collapse when you attempt to insert a needle into them. Every hospital visit meant more holes in my arm. My arm looked like a hair brush that had lost all of its bristles.

On this visit, I had a shunt inserted into my chest. The shunt is a semi-permanent tube often placed in patients undergoing intravenous treatment. The shunt allows the technician who is administering chemotherapy or drawing blood to do it through the shunt rather than poke a new hole in your vein each time. There are different types of shunts. Some are flat against your skin, and except for a small, round, flat thing resembling a Band-aid, are rather unobtrusive. The one they used on me, however, was particularly hideous looking. I had no idea what to expect, but when I woke up from the procedure and saw a twelve inch plastic tube dangling from my opposite breast, I was a little stunned. I felt like Medusa from Greek mythology, except that the snakey-looking thing was on my body rather than on my head. This thing would hide inside my bra for the next nine months, coming out only for showers and tube cleanings.

That was my third surgery in two weeks. It was a record for me. I was exhausted and ready for the next step.

Finally, with no more surgeries on the horizon, I was back home to recover from the awful tortures I had been subject to over the past two weeks.

This was an extremely difficult time for me. I was finally alone, too alone, with my thoughts and fears.

CHAPTER 5

Despair

One of the hardest parts about going through breast cancer was believing that I was going to die and nobody would care. The world would go on without me.

It was the loneliest time of my life.

Days went by and I spent my time in solitude, stuck to the couch like candle wax that melted on it and then cooled.

Over the next days and weeks, those two nasty little words, "Invasive" and "Aggressive," that I had read on my chart when I received my diagnosis came back to haunt me.

Remembering a scene from "Star Trek" where little alien creatures were introduced to a victim and were allowed to crawl around their body looking for openings, I imagined cancer cells resembling those little bugs, crawling around inside of me invading my bloodstream and working their way toward my vital organs.

I lived in fear that every new pain was going to be my demise. Even a simple headache screamed "BRAIN TUMOR."

Even though the doctor said I had "garden variety"

breast cancer, it was advanced—which in my current state of mind from three surgeries, needles, and drains—meant I was going to die.

I had a garden once, and I saw the life choked out of it from overgrown weeds. This cancer was a huge overgrown weed.

Despair hit me like a heavy rock in an avalanche. I wondered if I had done anything in my life that mattered. I began to think about my legacy. I tried to make a list of the good things I had done in my life and couldn't think of a thing. I worried again, that no one would come to my funeral, except those I had wronged. I knew they would show up only to make sure I was really dead. All I could remember was that I had been so self-indulgent and self-centered that I spent my life only worried about me. I felt like I deserved to die.

Depression wrapped its ugly mouth around me and tried to swallow me whole. I was no longer the person I used to be.

I had been so used to getting up early every day and going to work. Dressing up and playing the role of superstar sales woman was something I lived for. I loved my customers and they reciprocated. I was competitive and tough.

Every morning, when I arrived at work, I immediately headed straight to the wall of honor, or shame for some, and compared my daily results to those of my peers. As long as I was number one, I was happy. I was usually happy. My average work day started at 8:00 a.m. and ended when I was too tired to go on. There were times that after a full day of work, I rushed off to school. But even on the days without class, I often got home after 10:00 pm.

Now I felt I was doing well if I got out of bed before noon. Occasionally, I wondered who would take my place at the top of the list. Most of the time though, I didn't really care. All I could think about was how I would never be normal again.

CHAPTER 6

It's a Family Thing

This could've been an awful time for me had it not been for the fact that I was surrounded by my family and friends. Even my dog, Gretchen, sensed something was wrong.

Usually Gretchen is her "Daddy's girl" and follows my husband Bill around like his shadow. She loves Bill. She gets jealous and makes quite a racket if he hugs me. But during my treatment, she followed me everywhere. She was unusually calm and stayed right by my side. I remember one day when I tried to walk up the stairs to my bedroom. I was exhausted and climbed one step at a time, very slowly. Gretchen took the steps at the same pace. I'd always heard that animals have a sixth sense about things. I believed it that day.

Breast cancer affects the whole family. Three of my five children were young and still living at home. Telling them was one of the most difficult things I have ever had to do.

Recently, I asked my youngest son, Micah, what he remembers about my ordeal with breast cancer.

He was only eleven-years-old when he heard about my

diagnosis. I didn't expect him to remember many details, but he did have one clear memory. He recalled the family gathered together in the living room watching a video. Bill and I sat together on the couch. He remembered looking over at me and seeing tears in my eyes. He couldn't believe I was crying over the movie.

He asked me, "What's wrong, Mommy?"

I answered, "The sun is in my eyes." He got up and closed the shades.

I continued staring at the television, my eyes still moist with tears. I couldn't imagine how the words were going to come out of my mouth, but Bill and I had talked about it the night before and now seemed like a good time.

I asked the kids, "Can we please pause the film? I have something to tell you."

Micah was the first one to respond by hitting the pause button on the remote. They all turned from the television and looked at me.

"Mommy's a little bit sick," I told them. "I have to go to the hospital to get some medicine."

I don't know exactly what I said next, but I do remember trying to put a positive spin on it. I didn't want them to think I had a chance of dying. Yet somehow, in spite of my words, they knew. The room grew dreadfully quiet.

My second youngest, Elijah, then thirteen, seemed the most upset. He came over to the sofa, sat down as close to me as he could. He leaned against me and put his head on my shoulder. A moment later, he turned and wrapped his arms around my neck and held on as if my life depended on not losing his grip.

Over the next few weeks he didn't say much, he didn't have to. Every time I left for my chemotherapy appointment, something you will hear about later, he would hug me on my way out of the door and say, "I love you." One time, I made it all the way to my car before he realized I was leaving.

He yelled out the window, "Wait, Mom."

I got in my car, but sat there until he came out. I rolled down my window and he reached in and hugged me. He whispered to me, "I love you." I backed out of the driveway and drove down the street, tears rolling down my cheeks.

Becky gets a hug before leaving for her first chemo treatment from son, Elijah.

My daughter Beth was fifteen when faced with this news. She surprised me one day, months later, when she presented me with a poem she wrote for her school poetry class. She had written it shortly after my diagnosis. Included in her poetry project was a photo taken in New York in 1993. It was a photo of me standing next to a young man on a bike holding up the thickest, strongest bike chain I have ever seen.

The day she gave me the poem, I cried as I read the most tender words imaginable. The poem was beautiful, yet sad and incredibly honest. It amazes me that this child, this young woman, had such an understanding and capacity for love at her tender age. I've read the poem so many times and it still brings tears to my eyes and an ache in my heart to think she had to go through all these emotions.

"I love you Mom" by Beth Olson

I thank God today that you are here.
So many have lost their lives to
the tiny terrors that take torch
to their healthy bodies.
Though it may be selfish,
While I thank God, I pray to Him:
"Please, don't take her away from me."
And is it selfish,
That while you have been weak,
I have held on?
Well, I will be strong,
it's your turn to hold on.
And one more thing...I love you Mom.

Becky in New York – 1993. Beth presented her poem and this photo to Becky during her treatment.

My oldest son, Joshua, was just turning twenty and was attending college at the University of Oregon. He is a brilliant child. He graduated Summa Cum Laude from his school. Josh has always been a positive influence on everyone around him. He was home that summer and never even once hinted that he thought I might not make it. His positive, quiet strength radiated toward me and I am sure it had an impact on my healing.

My oldest daughter, Tanya, was nearly twenty-three when I received my diagnosis. Sadly, she was living a very difficult life in Seattle so she was physically and emotionally removed from us.

My husband called her one evening and told her the news. I know that she was heartbroken, partly because she was afraid she would lose me, but mostly because her own difficulties stood in her way of being able to help.

My husband reminded me that though Tanya was not emotionally available to support me or the rest of the family, he felt that she truly was devastated by the news.

She finally came home a few months later. One night, while sitting on the couch together, she leaned into me and placed her head on my shoulder, like a young child, cuddling with me on the couch. Obviously very worried, Bill remembers how sincere and needy her voice was when she said, "Mommy, you are my rock." Tanya, a beautiful, fiercely independent young woman was at a very vulnerable time in her own personal life. I honestly did not mind her dependency on me.

I think that as mothers, we never stop being concerned about our children and my maternal instincts toward Tanya never stopped. I treasure how desperate Tanya was for my good health, my love and support for her, and my need to get well for her sake.

Having her here was difficult because she had so many of her own needs, but it helped me in many ways by giving me something new and outside myself to focus on.

One thing that became clear to me is that when mothers or parents become seriously ill, the fear of loss is often amplified in those family members who are caught in their own world of hardships or troubles. They are already feeling vulnerable and they fear losing someone who they can count on for support and love. They may not feel like reaching out, but I am glad my daughter did and I am happy I could respond to her concerns in ways that helped us bond closer together again.

Breast cancer also reaches out and touches the lives of more distant relatives and friends. I was amazed at the outpouring of support from cousins and other family members.

When a family is touched by this disease, sometimes it takes all they have to stay positive and continually provide care and nurturing of the patient. It is extremely difficult for one person to carry the burden alone.

CHAPTER 7

The Treatment

Finally, in May of 1996 the moment I dreaded most was upon me. I began chemotherapy.

I had no idea what to expect. I had seen movies about cancer treatment. "Dying Young," with Julia Roberts really stuck in my mind. She was the caregiver of a young cancer patient. The movie portrayed his chemotherapy treatments in a pretty vile way. He would go to the hospital for a treatment and then go home and puke his guts out for several days in a row.

I was not excited to be starting down that path. I tried to look on the bright side. I thought that maybe with all the puking I expected to do, I could lose some weight.

"So, there is a silver lining," I thought.

The day before my first treatment was horrible. Every moment I was awake, I thought about what was to come.

That night as the family was gathered to watch television, I was on another planet. I lay on the floor and thought only about tomorrow. I don't even know what movie we were watching. That same night, I couldn't sleep. I anticipated my treatment and all the sickness that was to come. "I have to make sure that I clean the toilet before my appointment," I told myself.

Later in bed, again I imagined tiny cancer cells crawling around in my body. I envisioned the chemotherapy on a search and destroy mission to single out each bad cell and choke the life out of it. I cried off and on most of the night. What if the chemo couldn't find the right cells?

I finally woke up some time in the middle of the next day. I managed to shower and dress. Bill had gotten up early and cleaned the house for me while I slept. He even remembered the toilets.

My appointment was drawing near and Bill went out and started the car. That was my cue that it was time to leave for the clinic. All the way there, I again sat in silence, staring out of the window. I was so lost in my thoughts that my usual chatty persona all but disappeared.

Bill was worried about me. He had no idea how to help bring me out of my depression. He did know, however, how to reach into my heart. He simply reached over and put his hand on my knee and patted it gently, a gesture I will treasure forever.

That gentle pat gave me new strength. I knew I was not alone and half way to the clinic, I had a new vision. I decided to become one with the chemo and join forces with it. If it had any chance at all of finding those roaming cancer cells, it needed my support.

We arrived at the clinic and—with my new resolve—I threw open the car door and jumped out. I walked, head held high, quickly into the building, with Bill on my heels. I decided right then that I would just get this over with and get on with life.

I was on a mission.

We entered the inner office and checked in. When the nurse called my name, my heart pounded in my chest. This was it. Together, the chemo and I would destroy those little buggers.

I entered the specially-equipped treatment room and I took a good look at the place I would visit every three weeks for the next nine months of my life.

The room resembled a large industrial living room. The walls were a boring off-white and the room smelled of rubbing alcohol. The white linoleum floor with blue and gray speckles was clean enough that if you dropped your food on it you would not even hesitate to pick it back up and eat it. My kids call that the, "ten second rule."

Blue vinyl recliners knelt all around the edge of the room, each waiting to hold a victim in their lap. Each chair had one of those tall rolling stands designed to hold the IV drip bag, placed nearby. I pretended the stands were well trained, disciplined soldiers, lined up ready to help me win this battle.

The people in the chairs, some old, some not, looked sad.

Not much laughter in this room.

The only chatter in the room was in the corner at the nurse's station. The nurses talked among themselves as they prepared the special mixtures that would pump hope into the lives of the cancer patients.

I took my place of honor near the window. With Bill in the chair next to me reading a magazine, I closed my eyes and said a silent prayer. I was ready to begin the battle.

Using my shunt, or "plug," as I called it, the nurse connected me to an IV drip that, for the next two hours, slowly filled my veins with sugar water and steroids.

The mixture silently dripped into me. I closed my eyes again and pictured the little soldiers—the army—entering my bloodstream to save my life. My body got heavier and heavier as fluid continually entered my veins.

I was deep asleep when I heard the sound of someone, probably the nurse, handling the instruments on the tray next to my chair. I stirred and opened my eyes. There she was on a stool positioned right in front of me with a giant syringe full of bright red liquid. My veins were so full already, I couldn't imagine room for anything more. She took the huge needle and poked it into the shunt and slowly pushed the fluid into my veins. That fluid contained the army that would be released to carry out the secret mission that I had devised in the quietness and stillness of my heart.

My first battle was over.

Only eleven more to go.

• • •

On the way home from that first treatment, surprisingly, I felt great. Those steroids had really done their job. I felt like I could tackle the world. I had so much energy I wanted to go play.

My husband and I, remembering the words from the nurse—that I would be totally bald by my next treatment—decided to stop at a wig shop on our way home. We bounced around the aisles while I tried on every color and style imaginable. We had fun.

Finally, we settled on a bright red, "Peggy Sue," wig. This was particularly fun because I am a brunette.

"Why not," Bill said. "You're going to lose your hair anyway, might as well have some fun with it."

"Maybe chemotherapy won't be so bad after all," I told him.

I was so energetic and pumped up that I felt all my worries disappear.

When we got home, I called and invited some friends over to watch a movie when they got off work. The women showed up at my house around 5:30 p.m. After a round of hugging and words of kindness, I gave them a tour of our remodeling project that was still underway.

We finally settled in with our microwaved buttered popcorn and glasses of wine (I had water) to watch our agreed upon chick flick. We put "Waiting to Exhale" in the DVD player.

Everything was going along just fine and Whitney was just getting ready to exhale when it hit.

The wonderful aroma of buttered popcorn didn't smell so wonderful anymore. I moved pretty quickly off the couch, tripped over various legs stretched out in front of the sofa and made a mad dash to the bathroom.

My friends, worried about me, decided it was time to leave.

I lived with my head near the toilet for the next forty-eight hours. It was a good thing Bill had remembered to clean them.

I couldn't quite vomit, though I felt like I would any minute. The food my step-mom brought over to feed my family was appreciated but it made me gag. It was best if I just stayed in my bedroom near the bathroom, away from the smells.

• • •

I continued to feel the affects of the chemo over the next week or so. I was amazed at how something that was supposed to heal me could make me feel like giving up. It completely zapped my energy. Immediately my interest in socializing dropped to nothing. The idea of shopping, something I loved to do, sounded like a chore.

Life was going on without me. I just wanted to feel sorry for myself. Sleep was now the highlight of my day.

My chemotherapy was so strong that I could only go in for an injection every three weeks. The doctor said it was the strength of this type of chemo that would cause me to lose all my hair after the first treatment. By my second injection, I could expect to be completely bald.

Oh happy me. Middle aged, overweight and bald. How lovely. It was a good thing I had already made the trip to the wig store.

• • •

Time went by, the world went on and I sat at home waiting for my hair to fall out.

One evening, while sitting on the couch, depressed and expressionless, staring at the television set, my fifteen-year-old daughter, Beth, and her two best friends decided it was time to do something.

They all disappeared into the next room and began to whisper. I knew they were up to something but I had no idea what they were plotting and scheming about. They came back in and told me they were running an errand and they'd be right back.

They came home about twenty minutes later. I was still stuck to the couch when I heard the engine shut off in the driveway. They came in and quietly opened and shut the door. I heard them as they tip-toed into the next room.

Finally, thinking how clever they were, they came around the corner and plopped themselves down on the couch, one on each side of me and my daughter on my lap. Beth took my hand and said, "Mom, since your hair is going to fall out anyway, you might as well see what it would be like to be a blonde."

Beth pulled a box of blonde hair coloring out of the bag. My eyes got watery. I laughed and told them they were crazy but I was delighted at their wonderful impulse. I had tried the redhead look with my wig. Blonde would be fun.

We spent the next few minutes giggling and laughing. They draped a towel on my shoulders, made me hang my head over the sink and began squeezing the mixture onto my hair. Twenty-five minutes later—and still laughing—

they hung my head over the sink again to wash out the goo. I was wearing my old, faded yellow sweatshirt which completely soaked up the water as it ran down the back of my neck. I was drenched and cold, but happy.

They wouldn't let me look in the mirror until they combed out my hair and blew it dry. Finally the moment came and they marched me into the bathroom to see the vision of loveliness.

What a shock!!!

My hair was no longer the dark brown I had been used to. Nor was it the blonde I expected. It was the color of creamy tomato soup—light orange!

The color wasn't me at all, I decided too late, but I enjoyed the attention from the girls. Besides, my hair would be completely gone within the week. It was a hoot and the most fun I'd had since I started treatment.

Even my husband appreciated how this event seemed to snap me from my thoughts, if only for an evening.

The next few days went by, same as always, with me still waiting for my hair to fall out.

Finally, on the thirteenth day since my treatment began, I went to bed, wondering if tonight was the night.

It was!

At 3:00 a.m., I woke up, spitting and trying to wipe the hair from my mouth. I turned on the light next to my bed and to my horror, saw that my pillow was covered with long strands of tomato-colored hair.

I ran my fingers through my shoulder length hair and literally hundreds of strands came off in my fingertips. I panicked. I knew the end was near. I ran to the bathroom to look at the damage, expecting to see a giant bald spot. I didn't. At least not yet. The rest of the night was quit fitful.

The next morning, the sun light streaming through my window highlighted the fallen hair on my pillow. I bolted straight up in bed and gasped, "What do I do now?"

I remembered something that I had forgotten since the beginning of my ordeal. I'm tough. I can handle anything I set my mind to, and I decided that I could handle this. I made the decision I would simply shave my head. I would rather it be short so that when it fell out, I wouldn't be so aware of it.

For the next few hours, I agonized over actually shaving it. I couldn't imagine being bald-headed in addition to the dangling tube, swollen arm from the lymph node surgery, and lopsided breasts. However, the thought of watching it fall was even more dreadful.

Shaving it is not a big deal, I decided. This is something I could even do myself. I searched in the bathroom cabinets and finally located the shears, but I could not bring myself to actually plug them in.

I grabbed a cup of coffee, and sitting in my bathrobe at the kitchen table, I opened the yellow pages and scoured the pages for a beauty salon near me. I found the page and identified several nearby salons and began calling them to see what they would charge to shave my head.

With each salon I called, I explained the situation and told them I couldn't stand to watch my hair fall out, but I didn't have the guts to shave it myself.

Most of the receptionists either did not understand, or simply didn't care. They merely quoted rates and hung up.

I almost gave up and decided to shave it myself when I found a wonderful salon near my home. The man on the other end of the phone was so kind and told me to come by the salon later that day and they would see what they could do to help me.

"No charge," he added.

As my appointment drew near, I quickly showered and put on my very comfortable—and very ugly—green sweat pants with paint spots, and a green plaid button down shirt. I found that pulling shirts on over my head was still difficult. My arm was quite swollen from the lymph node surgery.

I didn't wash my hair or bother with make-up. I was a mess and I didn't care.

I considered taking a brown paper bag, with eye holes cut out of the front, with me to the appointment so I could leave the salon incognito, but I could not find one bigger than a sandwich bag.

I drove to my appointment with tears in my eyes. This wasn't going to be fun and I fully expected to walk out of the salon even uglier than I was going into it.

However, as I entered the salon that afternoon, the same wonderful young man that took my call came out from behind the counter with a big smile on his handsome face.

He said, "You must be the special lady we've been waiting for."

Suddenly, I wished I had paid a little more attention to my choice of wardrobe.

He extended his arm to me and walked me to the back room where the owner of the salon would take care of me. I felt like a bride in a sweat suit. As he escorted me, he told me that his mom died of breast cancer. He understood what I was going through. We walked slowly so we could continue the conversation. He said he'd pray for me.

Once I was seated on my throne, he went back to his station and came back with a little cup of "Jelly Bellies" to cheer me up.

When the owner of the salon came over to meet me, I was so impressed. He listened to my story and agreed to cut my hair very short. He would not take money for my haircut, nor would he completely shave me. He decided he would cut the sides very short, like a boy, but he would leave about an inch on the top.

"No one leaves my shop without style," he said. "Even if only for a few days."

I will never forget his kindness.

CHAPTER 8

A Wig and A Song

The next night, which by now was about two weeks after my first treatment, I decided to do something crazy. I was beginning to feel better. My energy level was coming back and I knew that I only had a few days left with any hair on my head. So I called my cousins and told them I was ready for a night out.

I put my new wig on over my very short hair and met them at a local Chinese restaurant. We had a long dinner and then moved to the Karaoke bar.

I love to sing. Karaoke is my moment in the spotlight. Since I was no longer in the spotlight at work, this was a good alternative.

As the night rock and rolled on, I sang, and sang, and sang. One thing I didn't expect was that my head got so hot under my wig that I started to perspire. The club was hot and believe me, it wasn't from my singing.

I excused myself from the group to go to the restroom. My plan was to wet a paper towel and in the privacy of a stall, remove my wig and wet down my head with cool water. With my thinning hair, I thought that would do the trick. However, my friends noticed I was gone for sometime and they were afraid that I was sick and came in to search for me.

The mob entered the bathroom yelling out, "Are you all right?"

I responded from inside the stall, "I'm fine, I'll be out in a minute."

I came out of the stall with the wig back in place, but my face was clearly red and I was still sweating.

My cousin, tiny, cute blonde Sonja, looked at me and guessed it was the wig that was making me hot and urged me to take it off. They all chimed in and one of them said, "I bet your hair is adorable. We're family, you have to show us."

I was embarrassed. I still had hair, but not much of it. They had not seen it yet, but I reluctantly took off my wig. It looked gross. My face was sweaty and I had wig indents on my head.

My friends were amazing. I was overwhelmed by their kindness and encouragement.

"You look great!" Sonja said.

She got out her comb, wet down my hair and reached up from her tiny 4'11" frame, and re-styled it. Her first task was to get rid of the indents on the side of my head.

They all told me how much they loved my short hair and said it looked so much better than the wig. Whether it did or not, who knows, but they blessed me that evening with their kindness.

I tucked the wig into by purse and boldly walked out of

the bathroom and back into the Karaoke bar. I sang my heart out with "Wedding Bell Blues."

Over the next few days, I continued to lose hair at an astounding rate. I found that if I combed my hair on top of my head just right, you couldn't see the bald spots. I gained new respect for men who do that funny looking comb-over thing.

I had joined the club.

• • •

On the seventeenth day since my first chemotherapy treatment, my husband and I got up early on a bright sunny morning, dressed and drove to the farmer's market near our home in Beaverton, Oregon.

We spent all morning examining the goodies at the booths. We managed to load our arms with bags of fresh produce, pasta and desserts and were visiting the lettuce stand when the wind suddenly gusted.

I was shocked when I saw hundreds of little strands of hair flying off my head. It grossed me out even more than when my dog shakes her body and her hair flies everywhere. I couldn't believe what I was seeing. I dropped the lettuce from my hand and told Bill, "We have to go now!"

We made a bee-line for the car, shedding a trail of hair behind us. Losing my hair was already difficult, but to be so embarrassed in such a public way was downright humiliating.

I had tears in my eyes and a pain in my heart.

CHAPTER 9

Bald is NOT beautiful ...at least not yet!

The next morning, groggy from crying all night—still humiliated and not looking forward to this day—I got up to shower. Bill was still sleeping.

Quietly slipping into the bathroom, I disrobed and turned on the hot water. I took another look into the mirror before I shut the door, I didn't like the view.

I had no idea it was about to get even worse.

I stepped into the steaming hot shower like I did every other morning of my life. But this time was different. Nothing could have prepared me for this moment.

The water hit my head and what little hair I had left slid off my head, down my body, and lay in a pool in the bottom of the tub. I shrieked. Bill, startled from his deep sleep, got out of bed and ran into the bathroom to see if I was OK. I was standing there in the tub, naked, bald and sobbing hysterically. He looked heartbroken. I had never been this distraught in front of him before. As he looked at me, he never let on, through his eyes or his smile, how totally disgusting I looked. He simply grabbed a towel, gently wrapped it around me and hugged me. We stood in total silence, except for my deep sobs, and he told me he loved me.

When the sobbing stopped, he gently said, "Honey, get your bathrobe. I'll clean up the mess."

I turned away from him and turned toward the mirror. I was horrified. I couldn't move. The feeling I had in the pit of my stomach when I saw myself for the first time, naked, with no hair, was unquestionably the most humiliating thing I've ever experienced.

The hideousness of the bald head, two extremely different size breasts, a tube hanging out of one of them, dangling down to my waist was more than I could handle. I hadn't lost enough weight to make even a slight difference in my physique.

I felt like Humpty Dumpty, broken, bald and round. My head looked like a giant egg. It was pure white, and being of Greek decent, it was a pretty big contrast to the rest of my face and body that tanned easily and held the color for a long time. To make it even uglier, I had a few tufts of hair still attached, one in the back of my head and one behind each ear. I could have simply pulled them out with my hands but I was frozen in place. I looked like a creature from "Night of the Living Dead." I felt like one too.

A few moments later, as I regained my composure, I was reaching up to give those tufts a tug when Bill turned toward me. He stopped me in my tracks and asked me if he could do the honors.

I said, "yes," and cried again.

He handed me my robe and suggested I go downstairs. The timer on the coffee-pot had been set the night before so the coffee should be ready, he told me. It was a beautiful, crisp, sunny morning. He encouraged me to enjoy a few moments of peace on the patio, with my coffee, and said he would be right down.

I put on my robe as he got the hair clippers out of the cupboard. I took advantage of the offer and went downstairs, glad the children were still asleep, poured a cup of coffee, hands shaking, and quietly went outside onto the patio. I wondered how dare the sun shine on such a dreary day.

I had no idea why Bill felt the need to do this outside, but I was glad he did. There was no mirror to remind me and the glass windows were too high up to allow a reflection. I didn't touch my coffee.

Bill came down a few minutes later with the electric barber shears that we had used so often on the boys. He plugged them into the exterior outlet and asked me to stand in front of him. He gently turned me to the best angle. He hit the "on" button, and the shears began to hum. Within seconds he had shaved all the remaining tufts from my head.

Then, before I could turn back around and face him—and without any warning whatsoever—he turned the shears on himself and shaved his head.

I couldn't believe it. He had beautiful thick dark hair that was suddenly lying on the cement floor of the patio.

He shed it for me. I cried again.

I decided right there and then that any bad deed Bill had ever done was totally forgiven and forgotten. He had just opened up a bank account at the "Brownie Point Bank" and his deposit was huge. He had racked up enough points in that one simple gesture to last the rest of his life.

He spent the rest of the day building up more points as he waited on me hand and foot, did the laundry, cooked meals, all the time trying desperately to ease my pain.

Becky – shortly after her hair fell out.

Elijah, Micah, Bill, Beth and Gretchen (the dog) right after Bill shaved his head.

CHAPTER 10

The Hat

During the next several weeks, I sank into a deep depression. Every glance into the mirror and sight of my bald head reminded me how sick I was. I didn't want to go anywhere unless I had to. When I did have to go out, the scarf on my head and the sadness on my face told people I was sick.

One time, I was invited to attend a meeting at a local restaurant. I was hesitant to go out, but since I hadn't gone anywhere in a while, I decided to make an appearance, as ugly as it was. With my head completely covered by a scarf, I left for the restaurant.

The restaurant, The Old Country Buffet, was a very popular place for lunch. There always is a long line at lunch because they have such a huge selection of food available. This was a typical day, crowded and noisy.

I finally got through to the front of the line, paid my fee, and headed toward the food tables. This was one of my rare excursions out in public with my bald head and somehow I thought that with my head covered by a scarf, I could trick people into not noticing.

I was wrong.

I was carrying my tray filled with all my favorite comfort foods, chicken, mashed potatoes, and macaroni and cheese, to my table when I noticed two elderly women sitting next to each other, staring at me as I walked by.

One of them nudged the other with her elbow and said loud enough for me to hear, "Poor woman, I'll bet she has cancer."

I felt my face flush with anger. I couldn't wait to get home. I hated being the focal point of someone's pity. I hated being talked about me like that.

• • •

The chemotherapy was getting worse. I felt sicker with each treatment. My nausea lasted longer and my energy level dropped further. I didn't realize that the reason I needed to wait three weeks between treatments is because my white blood count needed to return to a level that was safe. My doctor confirmed that it usually takes about three weeks to even get close to normal.

Then I had another treatment, and it dropped even lower.

This process effected my immune system and about every other system in my body. My teeth began to deteriorate, I quit having regular periods and I began to have hot-flashes.

It wasn't the cancer that would kill me. I might not survive the treatment.

It seemed as if nothing was functioning normally. My body was falling apart and all I could do was lie on the couch and try to hold myself together.

• • •

Then, on July 4, 1996, Independence Day, my good friend Patty called to see if she could come over to see me.

It had been about five weeks since I lost all my hair. I wasn't excited about seeing anyone. I didn't even go outside that night to watch my kids set off fireworks. But I really liked Patty and I hadn't seen her in a long time. So, hesitantly, I said, "Yes."

Patty arrived about an hour later. When I opened the door, she was standing there smiling her big beautiful smile. She had a brown paper bag in her hand and it crinkled next to my ear as she hugged me.

I asked her, "What's in the bag?"

She said, "Dennis wanted to give this to you himself, but he's afraid you might not take it the right way, so he made me do it."

I had no idea what to expect, but I had a feeling it would bring a smile to my face. Dennis, Patty's husband, is a crazy and wonderful man.

Patty took me around the corner into the hall to share this very private moment with me.

She held on to the package and wouldn't hand it to me until I agreed that I would take it as a token of their love and see it with a sense of humor.

Finally, relenting to her request, she handed me the bag, "Sorry it's not wrapped," she said.

"I don't care, but I sure am curious," I said as I carefully took the bag from her.

I opened the bag and looked inside. I stared at the object for a moment, not quite sure what I was seeing.

Suddenly, my eyes lit up and I felt a lump form in my throat. I ran into the bathroom, pulled the scarf off my head, pulled the gift out of the bag and placed it on my glowing white orb.

The funny little white baseball cap, with stick figures of bald headed people and the phrase "No Hair Day" graced the front of my head.

For the first time since my nightmare began, I was able to smile back at my reflection in the mirror.

I could see that this hat was not just a hat. It would be my lifeline. That silly little hat completely transformed the image in the mirror.

Maybe the mirror could be my friend after all.

• • •

The next day, I woke up early and got out of bed. I had tremendous energy, more than I'd had in a long time. I found new enthusiasm for life. It's crazy that this simple little hat gave me something to look forward to.

And I couldn't wait to try it out!

I quickly showered and put on some make-up for the first time in a while. I looked in my closet for the perfect outfit to wear on my first venture back into the world. I settled on a little blue and purple flowered dress.

After dressing, I proudly pulled the little white hat out of the brown bag where it spent the night. I went to the bathroom mirror and again placed this hat on my head. It looked even better in the morning light, especially with a little color on my face. I turned sideways to look at it from every angle possible. It didn't hide the fact that I was bald, but I just knew I could do this. I was re-born.

I decided right then that I could proudly face the world with courage and a good laugh.

With everything in order, I grabbed my purse, my keys and my grocery list. I went outside and got in my car. Pulling the visor mirror down, I looked one more time, just to make sure that nothing changed when I left the safety of my home. It hadn't. Once again, I smiled. I started the ignition, backed down my steep driveway and slowly drove down the street, still smiling. It was a new day.

I was feeling great until I pulled into the grocery store parking lot. I began to have second thoughts. I wondered if I was really ready for this. I said a prayer and decided I would never be more ready.

With all the resolve I could manage, I confidently opened the door and emerged to reclaim my place in the world. Making my way to the store entrance, I paused and entered through the automatic door. I held my head high using my best posture.

I was a princess, after all.

I grabbed a cart and began wheeling my way through the aisles. Amazingly, no one paid any attention to me, and except for the occasional smile from a passer by, I would have thought I was invisible.

Again, I thought, "I can handle this."

When my cart was full, I proceeded to the front of the store. There was only one check-stand open and there were two or three people in line. I slid in behind a young man. He may have been in his early twenties. He wore brown cut-off shorts and no shirt.

As I waited my turn, the line began to fill in behind me. I stood behind him for a minute or two admiring his bravery for standing there half naked. It's funny how only a man would wear his pant size on the outside of his pants. Thank goodness ours are hidden.

He must have sensed my staring at him because for some reason, he turned around and looked at me. Surprised, he said, "Cool hat lady, but why did you shave your head?"

"I didn't shave it. Captain Chemo did," I said, smiling back at him.

Clearly, he was embarrassed as he quietly responded with, "Oh," and turned away from me.

The people in the line became deadly silent. No one spoke. I felt horrible. The tension was so thick, it was like swimming in a jar of olive oil. I could hardly breathe.

This was my big moment to reconnect with my sense of humor, and I blew it. The poor guy almost died right in front of me. I wanted to abandon the groceries that I spent so long collecting and run to my car.

A few seconds later he slowly turned back toward me and asked, "Is it working?"

"So far, so good," I said with a smile and a huge sigh of relief.

You could almost hear the applause in everyone's heart. When it was my turn to pay, the cashier said, "Wow, what a great attitude."

I told her, "It's the hat."

She asked, "Do you mind telling me what kind of cancer you have?"

"I had breast cancer, but it's gone."

For me, saying my cancer was gone was a huge step. I had not, up until that very moment, acknowledged that I was healed. That was also the exact moment that I knew I would survive. My heart raced at this new revelation.

She went on to tell me her mom had recently been diagnosed with breast cancer and was just starting chemotherapy. Her mom was worried about how she would deal with her hair falling out. She asked me where I got my hat. I pulled the hat right off my head—in front of God and everyone to check the label inside, exposing the same bald head that I, only a day earlier, was ashamed to show to anyone.

I told her my story about how the hat changed everything for me. The dialogue lasted for several minutes and it seems that everyone in line got involved with our conversation. We were laughing and they all congratulated me for being so positive. It was healing for me and for the woman behind the check stand. She decided, right then, that incorporating a little humor into her mom's life would be a good thing for both of them.

I believe that things happen for a reason. I am certain that the entire episode in line that day happened for the benefit of the mother of the woman working behind the counter.

• • •

This was the beginning of many astounding moments I experienced. I continued to tell my story anytime anyone asked about my hat.

When I went out in public, which was often, people no longer stared at me or talked about me—they talked TO me.

I no longer held my head down or felt saddened by my situation. I was healing more every day, emotionally, physically, and spiritually. I never felt more alive.

My hat truly saved my life!

Becky – donning her special hat.

Becky, with daughters Tanya (L) and Beth (R) – 1997, one year after diagnosis.

PART 2

Inspirations for You, the Survivor

CHAPTER 11

Sister Lister

One night, shortly after my diagnosis, I was lying in my bed thumbing through stacks of magazines when an article caught my eye. Unfortunately, I didn't pay much attention then to the author, or I would be giving her credit now, but the subject was of interest.

Struggling with a life threatening illness, a woman had made a list of things that were important to her. Her list included the things that she wanted to have or do sometime in her life. She described the desire to one day own a beautiful silk bathrobe. The beauty of the list, she explained, is that if she ever found the perfect silk bathrobe, she could justify buying it because, after all, it was on her list. I loved the idea. I had always been a list maker.

"Ah, a sister lister," I thought.

I began to envision such a list of my own and wondered what I would put on it. My list, I decided, would be called, "My list of things to do before I die."

I got out of bed to locate my day planner, the one that held my list of appointments that had been canceled since my diagnosis, pulled the pen out of its holder and flipped the planner open to a blank section, section #2, in the back. I didn't want to think too much about my list, I just wanted to write what came to mind just in case I had the energy one day to make some of those things happen.

I was surprised that right at the top of my list was, "Get my Degree."

That same night I added nine more things to my list. They were things I had often dreamed about, like spending time in Vermont at a bed and breakfast during the fall, singing lead with a band, taking voice lessons, visiting Italy and more.

Finding that getting my degree was first on my list came as a bit of a surprise. In my younger years, I didn't value school that much. After graduating high school in 1970, I had attended one year of business school in Seattle.

As I mentioned earlier, I met someone, got a job, dropped out of college to get married and have children while continuing to work full time. I didn't have time for school.

I continued to work through my divorce and second marriage in order to help support my new family.

Overall, it took me twenty-six years to decide to go back.

Many people have asked me why I went back after so much time. In 1990, when I first got hired at the yellow page company I currently work for, I was living in Medford, OR. I worked for the company in Medford for about a year when I had a chance to interview for a sales position in the Portland office. My boss and friend, Gary Gibson, encouraged me to apply for the Portland position because, as he put it, "It's one thing to be a big fish in a little pond, but to really shine in this company, you need to be a big fish in a big pond." Portland was certainly a much bigger pond.

One thing you could count on was my desire to shine. I had been a top sales producer in every sales job I'd ever had. I was a Tupperware sales manager and earned VIP status. I worked as Advertising Sales Director for the Medford/Jackson County Chamber of Commerce in Medford, Oregon and more than doubled their advertising sales.

I was currently a top producer in the Medford office for the yellow pages. I interviewed for the Portland position over the phone and much to my surprise, a few weeks later, got the job offer.

On my last day of work in the Medford office, in May of 1991, Gary took me to lunch to speak privately with me. After a good round of chit-chat, Gary looked me straight in the eye and said, "With your work ethic and drive, as long as you keep it up, you can write your own ticket."

Gary also knew that I didn't have much education beyond my high school diploma. He told me that if I really wanted to excel in the company, a degree would not hurt me.

He made me promise that when I got to Portland I would sign up for school and I would take "just one class." That promise haunted me for the next four years.

During those following years, I advanced pretty quickly through the sales departments moving from small accounts to larger accounts. By 1994 I was responsible for approximately $2 million dollars in annual revenue.

Finally, in December of 1995, as I began thinking about getting into management, I once again remembered my promise to Gary. I made an appointment to attend an open house at Marylhurst University in Portland to learn about their Prior Learning Assessment (PLA) program. This program was designed for adult learners. It allowed me to receive college credit for what I've done—and what I've learned from what I've done—through my life experiences.

Fulfilling my promise to Gary, I agreed to take "just one class" to determine if I was a good candidate for the program. I remember feeling a huge load lifted from me as I kept my promise from over four years earlier.

In January 1996, I completed my "one" class, found out I was a strong candidate for the program, and in February of 1996, just one month later, enrolled in the school and signed up for classes that would put me on track to earning a Bachelor's degree in Communications. I started regular classes later that month.

Gary is a very clever man.

My first regular class was "bonehead math" which in reality was college level beginning algebra. I was assigned to this level of math from a mandatory placement test. I have always believed that numbers and letters don't belong in the same equation. If you tell me that 2+2=4, I am OK, but if you tell me 2+N=4, I'm in deep trouble.

I had a great teacher and half way through my ten week class, I was actually beginning to grasp some of the concepts when I received my cancer diagnosis.

I was only two months into my degree program when suddenly I had a decision to make, and fast. Should I stay in school or quit?

Taking a leave from work was an easy decision. My doctor signed the papers and my short term disability was activated. Friends then encouraged me to quit school as well so I could stay home and focus on healing. That was not acceptable. I didn't like my circumstances and I didn't want to spend my day focusing on them. Also, knowing that math and I are NOT best friends, there was no way I was going to throw away the five weeks I already had completed and have to start over again later.

My decision to stay in school took about five seconds.

Once I began chemotherapy, I was too sick to go to class. With the teacher's permission, my friend Sharon, who was in class with me, agreed to attend the classes and then come over to my house the next day during her lunch hour to teach me what she had learned the night before.

For the next few weeks, we did our homework together and then she turned it in for me at the following class. The teacher worked with us and was willing to accept this arrangement as long as I made it back for the final exam. I did. We each received an "A" on our final. Sharon was a great tutor!

When my math class was finally over I was trying to decide what I should take next. With such a gloomy diagnosis—given only a 60% chance to survive past five years—I knew that if I was going to stay in school and get my degree, I had better hurry. I had a long way to go and the clock was ticking. I decided to use my time off from work to get actively involved in the prior learning program. I had already attended the class to find out if I was a good candidate, now I needed to enroll in the classes to learn how to do it.

I signed up for the class in September and spent the next four months writing essays. I picked up 44 credits during those four months.

I also realized that by attending the university, I had the opportunity to get at least one item on my list checked off. I signed up for voice lessons. I ended up taking three terms in a row. I'm not a great singer, but I had fun and learned something about correct breathing techniques.

My final project in my third term included arranging and singing a jazz rendition of the "Star Spangled Banner," and to sing an Italian Aria, in front of my teacher, classmates and guests.

I went back to work about six months later, but I continued working on my "list." Finally, seven years later I completed the most important item on my list. On June 14, 2003, I got my college degree.

I checked two other things off my list that same day. In 2001, my dear friend, Evan, was graduating from the same school. I decided to attend the graduation ceremony and was sitting among the audience of 700 friends and family members, listening intently to the three student speakers.

Sitting in my seat, I visualized being on that stage, not only as a graduate but as a speaker. That day, I knew I would speak at my graduation and added it to my list that night.

When classes began the following term, I began lobbying my advisor, Jeff Sweeney, and begged him to recommend me for the role of graduation speaker. I continued to do so for the next two years. He thought I was a little crazy, first for wanting to speak and second for starting to lobby so early. He suggested that I wait until my senior year to ask again.

I worked my way through my junior year and finally, when I registered for my classes as a senior, I asked again. Jeff agreed to start the conversation with the powers that be.

In the final months before graduation, I was beginning to get concerned. I hadn't heard from Jeff. I knew that if I missed this opportunity, I would miss it forever. It was on my list, so it had to happen, and I had only this one shot at it. I contacted Jeff by e-mail and asked in the subject line, "Is it time yet?"

Jeff quickly wrote back, "Soon."

More time went by and I wrote him again, "Is it time YET??"

He wrote back, "The nomination forms have just come out. I've placed your name on the list."

There was deafening silence for at least another month.

I finally contacted Jeff by voice mail one last time. I said, "Jeff, I haven't heard anything. I don't know if that means I was not selected or that they have not decided yet. Anything you could tell me would be greatly appreciated

Again, I waited.

Finally, just two weeks before my graduation ceremony, I received the call I had been hoping for. It was a Friday and I was sitting at my desk at work. The phone rang, but I was late for an appointment and I really didn't have time to answer the phone, so I let it go to voice mail. When I came back from my appointment and played my message, it was from the Dean of Admissions, Mary Lee King. She asked me to call her back within 30 minutes if possible or it would have to wait until Monday.

She gave no indication as to why she was calling, but I knew she was the person in charge of graduation ceremonies.

My heart was pounding as I picked up the receiver and began dialing her number. I was hoping I hadn't missed her. The phone rang and she picked it up on the second or third ring.

"This is Mary Lee."

"Hi, Mary Lee, this is Becky Olson. I'm sorry I missed your call earlier. I am glad you're still there." I had called her back with only seconds to spare. She was just getting ready to walk out the door when her phone rang.

Mary Lee responded, "I'm glad you called. You've been nominated and accepted as a speaker for graduation. Unfortunately, the wheels of education turn slowly sometimes. I'm sorry we've taken so long to get back with you. Are you still interested in speaking at graduation?"

It's a good thing she couldn't see me, because I had tears in my eyes as I said, "I would love to."

I had already written, re-written and delivered my speech many times to an imaginary audience. Over the preceding months, people watching me driving down the street probably thought I was a crazy woman. They could easily see I was talking to someone, but no one was in the seat next to me. I had a trick that I used if someone pulled up next to me. I would start tapping on my steering wheel, bounce my head back and forth and pretend I was singing to the radio. I don't think that it worked. They would just smile and nod, I'm sure, while thinking, "That crazy woman is talking to herself and trying to get me to think she's singing."

After the call from Mary Lee, I didn't care.

I was crying and my hands were shaking as I hung up the phone.

Over the next two weeks, I changed my speech several more times. I finally got it down to a one page outline. I practiced it in the new format several times and finally had it down, or so I thought.

Graduation day was upon me. I was in line waiting for my turn to walk on the stage. The auditorium was packed. As I got closer to the front of the line, my nerves got the better of me. The plan was that I would be called on stage just as the others before me, but when my name was announced, they would introduce me as student speaker. Then I would take over the lectern as the others stepped away and present my speech.

I was finally in the front of the line and waited at the base of the steps for my turn once again in the spotlight.

Suddenly, I couldn't remember my first sentence. Having spoken many times in front of audiences, I know that the most important thing in presenting a speech is getting off to a good start. If you have a strong opening, the rest usually flows naturally.

Forgetting my opening line at one of the most important moments of my life was not a good sign.

Fortunately, I was still out of sight of the audience and they couldn't see the panic on my face. Thank goodness I had my outline with me because as I opened my discreet navy blue folder and took a peek inside. It was right there and my memory returned.

On June 14, 2003, I stood before an audience of nearly 800 people, with only two thoughts: DON'T CRY, and don't forget my speech.

I opened my folder, just in case, and never looked down. I started with the usual stuff, thanking three of my teachers and my advisor, Jeff, all of whom were sitting on the stage behind me, then moved on to my personal story and how important it is to take baby steps toward your goals. I talked about passion and how short life is. I gave a graduation speech that was met with more applause and laughter than I would ever have imagined. One check mark.

I picked up my folder and walked the rest of the way across the stage, smiling at my professors as they applauded and smiled back, and picked up my diploma.

Check mark number two.

My third check mark came later than night at my graduation party. One of the goals on my list had been to sing lead with a band, but finding a band that would allow me to sing with them seemed unlikely. So my husband formed his own for my party.

He had been playing in a Beatle's Tribute band so he

invited some of the guys to play for the reception. They invited me to practice with them.

We practiced for a month and that night, I walked to the stage and took the center microphone. I belted out "Oh, Darlin" by the Beatles. The range was a little high, but I managed it anyway. I sang a couple of others too.

Bill told the audience—after I sang—that I had just completed one more thing on my list. They all cheered for me.

If I sang badly, no one told me.

Check-mark number three.

The next morning, I opened my day planner in the quietness of my kitchen table, and rather unceremoniously, but with a smile on my face, checked those three things off my list.

Becky crosses one more thing off her list as she graduates from Marylhurst University in June 2003.

• • •

There are two things you need to know about a list such as this. First, you want to include things that will take a while to accomplish. If everything on it is something you can do in a week, when the week is over, you have no reason to keep on living. Everything is done. Second, you never want to complete everything on the list. As you check one thing off, you need to add one thing.

As I placed the check marks next to the three things on my list that morning following my graduation, I added four more things. The first one is to get my master's degree. The second is to appear as a guest on the Oprah Winfrey show, third is to dance with Patrick Swayze (Okay, so I'm a dreamer!) All three are still unfulfilled, but perhaps someday they will happen. I do believe that with God, all things are possible. The fourth thing I added was to publish my book. The fact that you are reading it now will tell you that I have accomplished that task. Yes, indeed, with God's help.

I've checked a few other things off of my list in the eight years since its creation and up until the writing of this book. For example, I was nearly robbed in Italy, (Italy was on my list, not the robbing part), I've enjoyed the soaring bald eagles in Alaska where I was born, and was enchanted by the largest rolling sage brush I've ever seen while visiting Montana. I spent time in Vermont and toured New England with my husband (in fact part of this book including this sentence was written on that trip).

I am still building a library room in our home in

Portland, Oregon. I love books and need a place to house them all. I may never finish that goal, but it will be fun to try.

For sure, there will be at least one copy of this book on that shelf. I'll even sign it.

• • •

I encourage you to dream. No one knows how much time they have. Focus on living, make a list, check it twice and then start taking baby steps toward making the dream part of your life.

Becky and Beth in Rome, Italy – 2000.

LIST OF THINGS
TO DO BEFORE I DIE

CHAPTER 12

The 5H Club

I promised you in the beginning that if you were a breast cancer patient that you would hopefully realize that the best is yet to come. Well, here it is. If you missed your chance to join 4H as a kid, now is your chance.

Join the 5 H Club now: Hair, Humor, Health, Happiness and Hope.

First, Hair: IT WILL GROW BACK and probably better than before. As my hair finally began to come back in, at first it was a non-color, no pigment, but eventually, it turned darker brown than before. It was curly and much thicker than the hair I lost. It was months before it straightened out, but even then, it was thicker and better than before. But it wouldn't have really mattered. I didn't care how it looked, I HAD HAIR.

Second, Humor: Breast cancer—and particularly my hat—helped me recapture my sense of humor. When my hair first came back in, it was really too short to wear without some type of covering, so I either wore my hat or wig. I was thrilled at finally being able to wear the wig since I found it difficult to wear with my bald head. It was too scratchy.

I remember one time I was at an event wearing my wig over very short hair. It was just starting to grow and was only about a half of an inch long. A woman came up to me and said, “I love your hair!”

“Thank you. Would you like it?” I responded and pulled the wig right off my head and handed it to her. It really threw her for a loop, but we all got a good laugh.

Third, Health: When I speak about health, I'm not talking about diet and exercise. After all, at 5'3" and on the upside of 150 pounds, I don't feel qualified to talk about that. The only thing I know about fitness is that I need to eat less and move more. Or is it eat more and move less? I tend to get them confused.

No, I'm talking about emotional health. This includes having the desire for company, social activities, and the willingness to accept help from others.

A death threat such as breast cancer often is the one thing that shakes a person into re-evaluating their needs. Once we know that we are mortal beings and that we can't do it all alone, we begin to look at our old ways and try to find ways to change them. As you begin altering your lifestyle to include time for yourself and those you care about, you will find your energy level returning faster. Researchers have known for some time that people will heal faster when they are emotionally strong. There are many good books on emotional healing. The Bible is one such source. By completely giving your situation over to God, you will find strength you never knew you had.

Fourth, Happiness: I am doing what I love. I still have a

very busy job but I no longer work twelve to fourteen hours per day just to please my boss and gain personal recognition. I try to limit my work to ten hours maximum so that I come home and spend time with my family and projects that I love.

I finished my college degree in June of 2003, about the same time I finished the first draft of this book.

In rearranging my time and figuring out what matters, I found that what I really want to do is write and do public speaking. Breast cancer forced me to make these changes and they have been good changes.

Finally, Hope: With all the advancements in breast cancer treatment, there is much hope. As long as we have hope, we have EVERYTHING!

In October of 2003, I met a woman who told me she had been diagnosed with breast cancer and was given three months to live. Twenty-six years later she was telling me all about it. No one knows anything for sure. God is the creator of life and He will decide when it is time to go home. Never lose hope!

CHAPTER 13

The Gift

Oliver Wendell Holmes once said, "Cemeteries are full of people who died with their music still in them. Why is this so? Too often it is because they are always getting ready to live. Before they know it, time runs out."

One day, while walking through a cemetery, I thought about this profound statement. I thought about the "music" as being the passion for life and the blessings we were born to receive. I also wondered why we are always "getting ready" to live rather than just start living.

As I walked from tombstone to tombstone, I read about fathers, mothers, brothers and sisters, all of whom certainly had their lives cut short, regardless of their age or circumstance.

I wondered as I read each name, if their music died with them. I wondered what their music was.

It was a bittersweet moment. I was sad for them, but happy in my own realization.

• • •

The book entitled, *The Prayer of Jabez*, by Bruce Wilkinson, taken from the Bible in 1 Chronicles, 4.9-10, speaks of a warehouse full of shelves containing beautifully wrapped white boxes with red ribbons. The boxes contain the blessings that God has for each and every one of us. The warehouse is full of them because, sadly, we have not asked to receive them.

I think we have all had a peek inside our box. We have in some small way felt a tug or an inspiration to do something creative and wonderful, yet we ignore those longings.

We believe that only children can experience such dreams. We believe that we are being silly or foolish to try such nonsense. I believe that those subtle messages are a look at our blessings, our passion. Our music!

Leaving the blessings hidden in the box is not what God wants for us. We are to let our gifts shine. It is only when we share our gifts that we can truly feel blessed.

I had one of those very special "ah-ha" moments on January 29, 2003. I was driving to Salem, rehearsing a speech that I may or may not ever be asked to give.

I asked my pretend audience to imagine sitting at their kitchen table. In front of them on the table is a beautiful satin box with a removable lid.

I asked them to imagine their gift hiding inside the box. A gift from God that only they have seen. I asked them to do something so brave, so bold, that they would know that the courage to do so could only come from God:

"Take the lid off of the box
and throw that lid away.
Take your gift out of the box,
and put it on display."

I asked them to imagine what it would feel like if they could use that gift as a way to build passion in their lives.

As a small child, I used to twirl around my house in a ballet costume. I imagined being a ballerina on center stage. My parents gave me ballet lessons for a time, but, like kids so often do, I gave it up when it became too difficult.

As a young adult, I maintained my passion for dance. I taught disco. I gave that up when I figured out you couldn't make enough money to support the family. I still love to dance, but I feel I waited too long to do anything about it. Now I enjoy it through watching others, but how I wish I still danced.

• • •

While in college I read a book called "Zen and the Art of Making a Living" by Laurence G. Boldt. The author discusses how great it is to be able to make a living doing what you love.

"Imagine, if you could do anything you want and you knew you could not fail," says Lucy Martin in her workshop, "Now is My Time." What would you do? If you can turn that one thing into your life's work, you'll never feel like you are working. Life would be your playground.

Only a few people are brave enough to venture in that direction. I think it's because they know they are likely to starve and a lot of them do, but they go out with smiles on their faces.

Since my cancer diagnosis, I have spent a lot of time re-examining my life. I'm not unique. That is what happens to most people when faced with a life threatening illness. One thing I have discovered is that it is such a waste of time to wait until then to figure out what you should be doing.

What were you meant to do? What is the one thing that still tugs at your heart from time to time? Could it be your gift?

• • •

I urge you to listen to the calling of your heart. If you dream about doing something special, find a way to start. Just start and the rest will take care of itself.

As a Christian, I believe that things happen for a reason and we need to keep our hearts open to the call of God. I believe that we all have a purpose on this earth and that God gives us our passions so that we may find our purpose.

It is difficult to see now, but there is a reason that God chose to allow you to endure this disease. Perhaps it is your strength of character or perhaps it is to help you slow down, to find your gift, and learn to share it with the world.

As you read in the previous chapter, my passion is public speaking and writing. I recently found a way to live my passion—which I now believe will lead me to my purpose—to share the message of hope and encouragement to women and families suffering through this dreadful disease.

Illness & suffering are not thrust upon you by God or by an outside agency.

CHAPTER 14

Journal

I have never been one to keep a journal. I've never thought about writing my life in a book. Maybe I was afraid of what it would look like. Maybe I was too busy to make the time for it.

After my diagnosis, I kept a journal. Mostly dates and times. I didn't know why I felt it was important, at least not then, but I do now.

Without my notes, this book would have been much more difficult to write. Because I kept a log of significant dates and feelings, I had the blueprint in place to write this manuscript.

When I started, I didn't start out writing a book. I simply wrote a paragraph. One paragraph became two. Two became three. Before I knew it, I was a writer on my way to becoming a published author.

I took pictures of my bald head, not because I like the looks of it, but because I saw a photo of Gilda Radner in a book about her experience with cancer. I didn't plan to put it in a book when I took the photo, but I thought that it might be important to my kids one day. I had no idea at that time that it would end up in my final manuscript.

Writing helps me organize my thoughts and fears. It's not perfect, but it's mine. The beautiful thing about writing your story is that it is your story. There is no judge, no jury. It's pure and it is right. No matter the outcome, it is still your story. It is perfect.

Write!

PART 3

Help For You, The Friend!

CHAPTER 15

Out of sight, out of mind

Despair is perhaps the greatest tragedy of breast cancer. Loneliness and isolation so often accompany treatment, and left unattended, this can lead to despair. Despair causes lack of hope and without hope, we have nothing.

David Spiegel, MD, encourages cancer patients to build a strong bond of social support. He stated in an article titled, *Introduction to Cancer-Psychosocial Support*, "Cancer can be a very isolating experience. Friends and family may feel awkward about discussing cancer with someone who has the disease. Cancer patients are often removed from the flow of life, spending time getting treatment rather than at work or with family."

Andrew Kneier, PhD, Ernest Rosenbaum, MD and Isadora Rosenbaum, MA suggest that one of the strategies in their book, *Cancer Coping Strategies*, in which they list ten steps toward emotional well-being, that reaching out for support can promote well-being, thereby enabling the patient to feel more energetic and resilient.

These professionals understand the importance of support for cancer patients. In their work, they successfully communicate that message to people like you, who are living the trauma with someone they care about.

The work we do with breast cancer patients and their families through Breast Friends has given us the opportunity to find out about the difficult things that face the potential caregiver, the friend.

The most common concern is in not knowing what to do or how to help. We tend to back away because we don't want to hurt the patient's feelings or embarrass ourselves. Backing away is the worst possible action we can take.

Once we back away, we lose sight of the problem. We get back to our busy lives and once there, it is so easy to get caught up in the day to day routine of living. Meanwhile, the patient is alone and afraid. Backing away is indeed, not the right response.

• • •

Repeatedly, I hear that many patients experience a flurry of activity and support in the beginning. While the patient is in the hospital, people come to visit. You may have even been one of the visitors. You probably brought flowers and a card. You might have even offered to take care of her family during her hospital stay by cooking a meal or helping with day care.

All of this is wonderful but it is not enough.

Once the patient goes home to recover, the reality of her

situation is just beginning to sink in. You may think your job is done.

It isn't.

People believe, incorrectly, that since the urgency is over, the patient will be okay. What most people don't realize is that it is just beginning for the breast cancer patient.

Surgery is often the easy part. The aftermath of chemotherapy, radiation, lymph node surgery, and depression are the worst parts and often times, she has not even begun to deal with them.

Once home from the hospital, the patient will find that she has way too much time on her hands. She is often alone with her thoughts and many promises of help. One of the most common statements from her friends is likely to sound something like this: "Please call me if there is anything I can do to help."

It's a great offer and usually very sincere. The problem is most patients won't place that call. Yes, they need help but they don't want to be a burden, so they suffer alone.

• • •

Not only is backing away bad for the patient, it is also bad for you, the friend.

In 2002, I was working with a client. She saw the pin I was wearing on my lapel that represented the non-profit organization that I co-founded called "Breast Friends." She asked me to tell her about the pin. I shared with her the work we were doing with newly diagnosed breast cancer patients and their friends and family.

As I told my story, I saw her become teary-eyed.

I asked her, "Are you okay?"

"No, not really," she replied.

She went on to tell me that her dear friend and mentor, who helped her as she was just completing law school and heading toward the bar exams, had been diagnosed with breast cancer. Like so many, my client, busy with her own life and experiences, did not call her friend to offer assistance.

She thought about calling her—quite frequently in fact—but life got busy and she kept putting it off.

She told me that one day, while sitting at her desk, the mail was delivered and in it was the monthly industry newsletter for her area. As she read the newsletter, her heart was torn in two when she read the notice of her friend's memorial service.

Needless to say, my client was devastated.

"I never got to say goodbye," she tearfully confessed.

Clearly, staying in touch is important to not only the survivor, but to you as the friend.

• • •

Now comes the challenging part. How do you help?

I know from first hand experience how difficult it is to know what to do. When my friend Sharon was diagnosed in 1993, I had no idea how to help her. I was one of the invisible friends who offered to assist her if she needed me, however, I had no idea of what she might actually need.

Since she never asked for help, I assumed she was doing fine. I knew she had a husband and children who were caring for her. The problem with that is when the husband was at work, and the children at school, Sharon was alone with her thoughts and fears.

I learned through my experience, three years later, that the loneliness can be unbearable.

I realized I was not the greatest of friends to Sharon. I was embarrassed when she would come to the office for a visit. I didn't want to face her. I knew that too much time had passed and I hadn't done my part.

I would give anything to be able to reverse this situation. At best, I can learn from it.

When I was diagnosed with nearly stage III breast cancer three years later, Sharon knew exactly how to help me.

CHAPTER 16

So Much to Do... But What???

There are so many wonderful and easy things that can be done to help someone get through this difficult time. Please allow me to share with you some of the best things that happened for me that helped me in my transition from victim to survivor.

#1 – Call or Write.

One of the simplest, yet most important and meaningful things that you can do is to send a note or make a phone call.

Being home alone all day—every day—can be a very difficult thing for some women. For me, Ms. Social Butterfly, it was unbearable. I would sit at home and hope my phone would ring. When it did, it was usually someone trying to sell me long distance service, an alarm system, or satellite television. I found myself welcoming the intrusion. The only thing worse than that was the silence. When my friends did call, it was a tremendous boost to my spirits to know someone was thinking about me.

Remember too, the conversation doesn't have to be about cancer. It can simply be "I was thinking about you today" or "I was sitting at my desk and I saw an inspirational poem (or a joke) that made me think of you." You can then add, "I hope you get back here soon. We need you!"

Just start the conversation. Trust me, the rest will follow. She'll just be glad you called. Also, don't allow your personal embarrassment stop you from doing the right thing. If it has been a long time since you checked in with her, it is easy to tell yourself that you can't call her now—it's been too long. Make the call anyway. She will be so glad you called that all the time in between, when you were absent from her life, will vanish.

One time, we were giving a presentation to a group of 200 men and women about the importance of support and friendship. I was talking about the importance of staying in touch by phone and how it was the most meaningful thing you could do.

After the evening was over, a woman, who had been standing in the wings, waited patiently to speak to me.

As she approached, I could see in her eyes that she was experiencing some strong emotions. She told me through her tears, that the message she heard from us that night relieved years of guilt. I asked her to explain. She told me that she had lived out of the country a few years earlier. While she was gone, her friend was diagnosed with cancer. She was not in a position to return home and all she could do was call. She called her friend often, but she didn't feel it was enough.

Sadly, her friend didn't make it, and the guilt was more than she could bear. She wasn't able to be there for her friend physically.

After hearing our story, she finally realized that her many phone calls did matter. The guilt was finally gone.

Another way to stay in touch is through the mail.

Outside of my hat, probably the single most wonderful thing that happened for me was going to my mail box every day and finding at least one card or letter, sometimes several of them.

I had two friends at work that coordinated a letter/card writing event. Sharon sent out e-mail updates to the entire office and asked people to send me a card or letter. She gave my address on each e-mail.

The result of that effort was phenomenal. She sent out an update once a week so people would have multiple chances to write. With every update, I received cards for days after. I received cards from people I didn't even know.

My other friend, Heather, was on my sales team. She took up a collection from our other teammates and used the money to purchase a huge supply of get well cards and stamps. She had my teammates sign the cards all at once.

Every other day, she dropped one in the mail. These cards were often humorous and sometimes serious, but they all communicated the same message...we miss you and hurry back.

It's hard to feel alone when every other day you go to your mail box and find a card that tells you that you are missed.

#2 – Help with Chores - What A Mess!

One thing that happens when you go through chemotherapy is your energy level drops to nothing and it is so easy to stop caring about a lot of things.

During the nine months I spent on chemotherapy, I stopped caring about things like laundry, dishes, floors and beds. My house got worse and worse.

I spent my days sleeping on the couch or in my messy bed. I had worked full-time my entire adult life and sitting at home wasn't exactly what I was used to.

I was bored and sleeping helped me pass the time.

One day, Bill's cousin Candis called and asked if I minded a little company. I told her I was a little tired but said she could drop by. She then asked, "Do you have a CD player?"

"Yes," I said. "Why?"

She didn't exactly answer the question, but about an hour later she showed up with a stack of music CD's and a pair of rubber gloves.

I was puzzled.

She explained that the rubber gloves were so she could clean my house and the CD's were to supply her with background music, "Because I can't clean a house without music," she said.

"You can either relax and visit with me while I clean or you can take a nap. The choice is yours," she stated enthusiastically.

I thought about it for about three seconds. The nap sounded good, but then I remembered something my friend Theresa likes to say, "You can sleep when you're dead." I chose to visit. Besides, I had already slept enough to last me for a year.

Candis placed her CD's in the CD changer as she made her way into my kitchen. She scrubbed my kitchen and bathrooms, then she threw a load of laundry in the machine, stripped the beds and remade them with clean sheets. I couldn't believe it.

She did such a great job!

Her enthusiasm was contagious. Having her energy around me made me feel better. I found myself a willing participant in the clean-up project.

Before I knew it, I was straightening stacks of mail that had accumulated on the kitchen table and seemed to be taking over my life.

Eventually, I found the broom and knocked down the cobwebs in the corners of the room. My spirits were lifted and before I knew it my house was clean.

Had Candis asked if she could come over and clean my house, I would have said, "No, that's OK. I'm fine."

Instead, she simply asked if she could drop by for a visit. When she got there, she cleaned. A very clever woman, indeed!

• • •

Our lives are filled with many events, some memorable, some we'd rather forget. In 1996, the year of my diagnosis, I hired a contractor to put an addition on our house. We added 500 sq. ft. of family living space above the garage and added a stairwell from our family room.

The design originated on a napkin and was replicated

on official blueprints. It was a greatly anticipated and wonderful project.

As the kids were growing, their need for more space was growing and my need for quiet was growing.

We started the project in early April, before my diagnosis. I received several bids and made my choice. Supplies were ordered, contracts signed. Work began.

But the day I came home from the mammogram appointment with the surprise diagnosis, I knew the project had to be canceled. I decided we would postpone it until I was in a better mood.

As I pulled into my driveway however, I saw to my horror that the garage had no lid. The workers had already removed the roof and were preparing for the framing of the addition. I knew it was too late to cancel the project.

I couldn't believe how fast the project was moving. Trying to stop it now would be like trying to stop a train at 150 mph.

The good news was I would be home to keep an eye on the project. It's a good thing I was because they almost put a wall in the wrong spot.

The bad news was, the mess they created was enormous. The dust was so unbelievable. It was impossible to breathe and the mud through the house was unbearable.

My house was a disaster. But I wasn't working, so I had no funds to hire anyone to help me clean my house. Except for the fact that breathing was difficult, I didn't really care. I simply didn't have the energy to clean the mess.

Sharon came to my rescue again! She sent out an e-mail message at work directed at everyone in the Portland office.

She told them about my construction nightmare and asked people to give a donation to help me with my cleaning project. She knew I didn't have the energy to clean it, yet she knew that it was really bothering me.

I had no idea she had even started such a project. Imagine my surprise when she showed up at my house and delivered over $400 in cash along with the message that the money was to be used for window cleaning, blind cleaning, and carpet cleaning when my remodel project was done.

My project was finally completed in July. The money, which had been safely hidden in the bank, found itself on its way to becoming a clean start toward enjoying my new and improved home.

I opened the yellow pages, found someone for all three jobs, and set the appointments.

Because of the creativity of my friend and the generosity of my co-workers, I had enough money to complete all three tasks. My house was cleaned and we could all breathe again.

#3 – Make a Regular Date to Do Something Fun.

Watching a movie doesn't take a lot of energy and you already heard about how important humor is in helping a cancer patient cope. For me, finding humor is easy at the movies.

I love movies. I try to see all new movies that interest me early in their release, so I have a chance to see it before the ending becomes common knowledge. Going through cancer treatment didn't change my desire and having a friend who also likes movies helped me live my desire.

My dear friend and fellow movie enthusiast Patty (the

one who gave me the hat) gave me something to look forward to every week. I could count on her call every Friday morning to see what movies were starting that afternoon.

We picked out a standard "Chick Flick" and agreed to meet at a movie theater for the first showing of the movie we wanted to see. Being "chicks," it was pretty easy to agree on which film we wanted to see. We usually picked something funny.

We always arrived early so we could visit for a while before the movie started. It was a great time for us to bond, to bring her up to speed on my treatment, and then focus on the movie.

One thing that came as a surprise to both of us during this time was that I didn't usually feel like dwelling on my disease and though she always asked how I was doing that week, I didn't have to talk about it if I didn't want to.

Patty was excellent at respecting my moments of quiet and reflection. I discovered that there are times that I wanted to feel normal. C.W. Metcalf says in his book, *Lighten Up*, "I have cancer...cancer doesn't have me." By allowing me to not discuss it, Patty was honoring my desire for normalcy.

#4 – Be Consistent – Stay in Touch Regularly.

One time I was interviewing a cancer survivor for a research project that I was working on at school. She brought up a very interesting point. She told me that if you have friends that stay in touch on a constant basis, you don't have to spend every conversation explaining your disease and your treatment. They already know what you are going through and you only need to give a quick update.

The reverse is true, if people only call you once and then forget about you, you have to relive the agony as you explain, again, your circumstances with each new call.

Of course, you can always reject their calls but the option is being alone too much of the time.

#5 – Running Errands is a Great Way to Show You Care!

I love to camp, but only if I can be organized. With my job, I had not been able to take time off in the summer for over five years. Breast cancer gave me the opportunity to spend some quality camping time with my family.

My problem was I didn't have the energy for the organization part.

In August of 1996, my friend Patty knew I was going camping with my family and she called to see how I was doing with the plans. I told her—in tears—that I had decided not to go because I hadn't done any grocery shopping and I felt too sick and exhausted to do it.

She asked me to read my grocery list to her over the phone. At first I resisted, but she insisted. I read her my list. She went to the store and an hour later, she was at my house with groceries and a receipt. I wrote her a check, over my tear-stained checkbook.

Patty not only unloaded the groceries and helped me put them away, she helped me get things packed in the coolers.

My husband came home later, loaded the car with our camping gear and our totally organized coolers.

We had a wonderful time. At least most of the time.

Only two things went wrong on our trip. First, the location. It was very hot during the day and freezing cold at night. I have a new appreciation of what bald headed men go through. At night, it was so cold I couldn't sleep. I learned that when you plan to spend time in the cold, wear a hat to keep in the body heat. I had tried my scarf, but it kept falling off. Feeling sorry for me, my husband gave me his knit hat to keep my head warm.

Second, I failed to respect my doctor's warning about the sun. My advice to anyone who is on chemotherapy or radiation: when the doctors say stay out of the sun, they mean it.

My husband tried to set an example by sitting alone in the shade wearing a long sleeved shirt, top button buttoned, shorts and brown socks with sandals. He fell asleep in a lounge chair, in the ninety-degree shade under a large oak tree. He looked more like Forrest Gump than did Tom Hanks.

Anxious to renew my youthful tan, I however, stayed in the sun protected only by my bathing suit and my hat. I had no idea that some forms of chemotherapy make you extremely photo sensitive (meaning overly sensitive to the sun).

Boy howdy…I ignored the warning and lived in the sun for the entire weekend, unaware of the insidious sunburn I was wearing but not yet revealing.

This was quite a new experience for me considering my Greek ethnicity. I had spent many summers in the sun without any protection what-so-ever. In fact, I often used baby oil to attract even more sun. Usually the first day I would turn slightly pink, but it would turn a deep brown by the second day. I had no idea I could burn so badly.

Over the next few days, my burn deepened and became a

dark burgundy color. My skin finally peeled and even after three layers of peeling, I was still a deep purple color and it hurt.

Even the best burn ointment couldn't soothe the pain.

Eventually I turned normal again, but it took months of ugly and pain. I do not visit the sun any more without a very heavy sunscreen (good advice for anyone).

#6 – For Husbands and Lovers - Show Her You Care!
(warning, if you don't like reading about sex, skip this part).

Once I got over the fear of dying, I found that one of the hardest things about surviving breast cancer was wondering how the deformity would affect my sex life. I'd heard terrible stories about husbands who left their wives, boyfriends who broke up with their girlfriends, all because they couldn't accept the physical downside of breast cancer.

There is no doubt, breast cancer alters the contour of a woman's body and it takes a very strong man to accept it.

I count my blessings daily that I have a husband with a terrific sense of humor and a perverse imagination. You read how wonderful he was in Part One. If you were not convinced that he is special, perhaps this story will help you.

When I came home with gauze and drain tubes hanging out of my breast, I could barely look at myself. My husband, Bill, on the other hand, wanted to see it up close. He would look at me while I was nearly nude, examining the wounds.

He was fascinated at the size of my arm as it filled with lymphatic fluid. He sometimes stroked the back of my arm to test my reflexes.

Unfortunately, lymph node surgery can cause severe

numbness and I couldn't feel the strokes. But I knew in my heart that he was doing all he could to help me heal.

When my hair fell out, he rubbed aloe-vera gel on my head and chanted the mantra "be nice to bunny...be nice to bunny" (bunny was my nickname since my pregnancy with our first child).

With all my scars and lop-sided breasts I couldn't look at myself, so how could I expect more from him.

One night, as we cuddled in bed, Bill gently whispered in my ear, "I've always wondered what it would be like to be intimate with a biker chick. Maybe when you're feeling up to it, we can find out?"

"Do I look like a biker chick to you?"

"Yes and I love it."

The first time we were intimate was scary for me. I did not like to hide from him. But I decided that if he could pretend I was a biker chick, then maybe it would be okay.

I nearly dropped dead in my tracks when he said afterwards, "It was like I was with two women." He went on to explain that one had a tight, perky breast (the breast cancer side) and one with "a big one" (my normal side). He never let me feel ashamed of my body.

He continued throughout my treatment—and still to this day—to tell me I was (and still am) beautiful. He is, of course, over 50 and his eyesight is beginning to fail, but it works for me.

If other men could adopt the attitude he managed to develop, this world would be a better place. No woman should have to face this disease alone, but unfortunately, many men will allow them to. Perhaps they all need a little "biker chick" excitement in their lives.

Over the years since my diagnosis, I've thought about having reconstruction to make myself more "balanced" but I'm afraid my husband would miss the "other woman."

I do feel that men need support in this area. Bill is pretty special, but not all men can handle this situation with the grace that Bill showed. Just like some women handle their emotions easier than others, men will experience different emotional needs as well. There are support groups available for men as well as other family members who are having difficulty dealing with this issue.

Check with your local hospital for information on groups in your area.

• • •

I truly feel that the most important thing you can do to help someone through their crisis is to help them laugh.

A.H.H. Klein wrote in an article entitled, *Humor in Not-So-Funny Times*, "Constantly color your picture gray and your picture will always be bleak. Try adding some bright colors to the picture by including humor, and your picture begins to lighten up."

Brighten up someone's day, and your day will brighten up with it.

CHAPTER 17

Breast Friends

In August of 2000, while sitting in the hospital cafeteria with my friend, Sharon, we began discussing the deeper meaning behind being blessed with surviving breast cancer. Our conversation quickly turned to a discussion about what was missing in the area of breast cancer support.

What we soon realized, and agreed upon, was the fact that there was not much information available to the friends and family members of the breast cancer patient—information that would help them, help her.

We decided that day that we wanted to find a way to help breast cancer patients by teaching those around her how to be of assistance to her. We decided that day, August 22, 2000, that we would start a non-profit organization dedicated to helping breast cancer patients, by helping her friends and family members.

We started the process by registering the name, Breast Friends, with the state of Oregon. We registered the URL for a web-site, not yet built. All of this was accomplished in the first 24 hours.

With a big sigh, we phoned each other and asked...now what?

That question is still being asked and answers are still being discovered. Changes happen every day. But we are ready to do what God is calling us to do. We pray the "Prayer of Jabez" by asking God to bless us, to expand our territory, and to keep His hand upon us, that we may not cause harm.

He is blessing us by introducing us to many wonderful people that we would not have met otherwise. We are encouraged knowing that what we are doing is right and that our message is sound.

He is expanding our territory. What began as a dream is now a reality. We achieved our tax exempt status in November of 2001. We are speaking all over the country. We are building a network through other well-known cancer organizations such as the American Cancer Society and the Susan G. Komen Foundation.

We received our first grant in 2004. After three years of trying, we finally received funding from the Susan G. Komen Foundation. We were funded again in 2005 and 2006 and are now chairs of the Komen Co-Survivor program in Oregon and SW Washington.

We know that God is keeping His hand upon us by placing people in our path at the exact moment we need expertise on something. These "Jabizness" meetings bring incredible blessings to our organization.

I am living my dream. I am involved in public speaking throughout the country. My book is published. Life is good.

I can say that the hat truly has saved my life...**twice!**

(As we are working toward building and expanding Breast Friends, we have learned of other organizations with the same name, that have surfaced and though we are not officially or legally connected to each other, we are connected in heart and share a common purpose of bringing comfort to breast cancer patients.)

• • •

MORE ABOUT BREAST FRIENDS

Breast Friends: The friends and family network for support and inspiration.

Our mission: "Helping women survive the trauma of breast cancer...one friend at a time."

One in eight women will get breast cancer in her lifetime... The other seven will know her.

Our Goal: To teach those seven how to help her.

CHAPTER 18

Tips for Caregivers

The following is a list of ideas reprinted with permission from Breast Friends, Portland, Oregon. (Please visit www.breastfriends.com for more information.)

1. **Just Call to Chat.**
2. Hat Shower—give a shower for your friend. Have everyone bring a pretty, or fun hat.
3. If a co-worker is diagnosed, send out e-mail to your company distribution list and give your friend's address so employees can send cards and letters.
4. Take up a collection and buy a day of house cleaning, window washing, or carpet cleaning for your friend.
5. Cook a meal for her family on chemotherapy days.
6. Drop by with a milkshake.
7. Go to a matinee movie and/or to lunch.
8. Drop by to do some laundry.
9. Run some errands for her (grocery shopping, post office, bank deposits).
10. Get manicures and pedicures.
11. **Just Call to Chat.**
12. Wash her car.
13. Help with yard work (and chat while working).
14. Take her to hit a bucket of golf balls (depending on her level of strength). It's good exercise for her arm after lymph node surgery.
15. Arrange for a day of baby-sitting so she can rest.

16. Go wig shopping—try on crazy colors (the crazier the better).
17. Buy her a new shade of lipstick.
18. Invite her to a special lunch, bring out the fancy china and silver. Don't forget the linen napkins. What are you saving them for anyway? Celebrate your friendship and life.
19. Many restaurants have gourmet foods to go. Bring home her favorites and enjoy them with her in comfy clothes.
20. There is nothing better than the smell of warm bread, or the taste of warm bread with a slather of butter. Share the experience with her, and of course do the clean up. Slice it up and freeze it, so she can enjoy it later.
21. Bring over an assortment of herbal teas. Looking for a better nights sleep? Try chamomile. Need an afternoon pick up? Try hibiscus and rose hips.
22. **Just Call to Chat.**
23. If your friend likes to cook, bring over some fresh herbs. Many supermarkets are stocking them these days.
24. Ice cream sundaes are always in style. Bring over a few toppings and you have instant fun.
25. Create a fun "Do Not Disturb" sign for her to use if she needs some alone time. Great for that long relaxing bath or an afternoon nap. Don't forget a nice basket of bath products.
26. If you don't have time, pay a responsible teenager to do some mundane and tiring errands to take away some of the burden of chores.
27. Breakfast in bed is always a hit. Don't forget the flowers to brighten up the tray.
28. Take your friend for a new look. It's more fun to do it together. If she's up to it, try on some new styles of clothes together. A bald head goes well with punk styles. Pick something you would never normally wear and have a good laugh. Don't forget the camera.
29. Get a few wild temporary tattoos and have fun putting them in daring places.
30. Drive your friend around so she can more easily do her errands. It will take some of the stress out of errands and make them more fun at the same time.
31. Pamper your friend with a paraffin wax treatment. The warm wax does wonders for circulation and makes your hands soft and smooth. It can be used for sore, tired feet as well.

32. When you come to visit your friend, suggest she take a long hot bubble bath while you watch the kids, do the dishes, or just field the phone calls.
33. **Just Call to Chat.**
34. Before she loses her hair, dye it a color she's always talked about, or get it cut short and sassy. Encourage her to be daring by trying out some new styles or looks. Remember, it's only going to last a week or so.
35. Try art therapy. Not creative enough? Bring over a couple of coloring books and color crayons and help her feel like a kid again with color book therapy. It's a good time to talk and bring out the creativity even if she isn't an artist. Don't forget, it's okay to color outside of the lines.
36. If your friend is dealing with lymphedema you could hire a massage therapist that is specially trained to help relieve the pressure and help her relax.
37. If you like to do crafts, bring over the supplies and share your craft with your friend.
38. If you have a sweet pet that likes people, share them with your friend. Pets have special healing power. (Check for allergies beforehand.)
39. One way to pamper your friend is to shampoo her hair (or massage her head with lotion if she has no hair).
40. Oh Yeah… **Just Call to Chat!**
41. Finally, is she says no… Keep calling and offer to help again later.
42. Visit www.breastfriends.com for additional ideas.

Don't try to do it all. Take care of yourself too. Ask for help from others. People want to help. When someone asks you how they can help your friend, pass this list to them and encourage them to participate in one or more ways.

If you like what you've learned about Breast Friends and would like to get involved in supporting our mission, you can help us get our message out by:

1: Purchasing this book and learning new and practical ideas that you will be able to use should the need arise. If you are reading this now, you've probably already started down that path and we thank you.

2: Sending a tax deductible donation to Breast Friends, **8152 SW Hall Blvd, #301, Beaverton, OR 97008.** Your donations will help fund on-going projects.

3: Volunteering your time to assist in our efforts. You can reach us by calling **503.598.8048** or **888.386.8048** or visit **www.breastfriends.com.**

4: Becoming a "Pin Pal" and show your support to someone diagnosed with breast cancer. Visit our web-site at **www.breastfriends.com** to find out how.

Breast Friends is a not-for-profit, 501(c)(3), Federally tax exempt organization. Partial proceeds of the sale of this book will be donated to Breast Friends.

To order additional copies of this book, please visit:
www.beckyolson.com

We thank you for your support!

EPILOGUE

"Old Hat"

Bill finally lost the "other woman." Turns out he lost the first one too.

June 1, 2004, just three days after I sent my book to my publisher to begin the edits for the first printing, I found a suspicious lump while showering. Later that day a mammogram revealed a probable breast cancer tumor. Just two days later, on June 3, a biopsy confirmed it: Stage 3. Again! Round 2.

Following my lumpectomy after the first battle—when I still had breasts though very different in size, Bill encouraged me not to get reconstructed. He said it was like being with two women. With this second diagnosis, I made a much different decision. I'd had enough. I decided on a double mastectomy. By June 14, 2004, I was breastless. The "Girls" were gone.

• • •

For eight years following my first diagnosis, I thought the only thing worse than hearing that I had breast cancer, would be to hear that I had breast cancer AGAIN! I was wrong. I was an old hat at this. When diagnosed the second time in 2004, my thoughts turned immediately from "been there, done that" to figuring out how I would be able to hide my diagnosis long enough to get through the biggest speech of my life, the Susan G. Komen Survivor Luncheon at the Oregon Convention Center. I had been asked to speak at the event prior to my second diagnosis. I knew that with the luncheon coming up in less than three months, I would be in the heat of chemotherapy, bald once again and possibly too sick from chemo to stand before the audience of 1000 or so expected guests.

My doctor didn't think I should even consider giving the speech.

I changed doctors.

I immediately went through a double mastectomy and began chemotherapy. I made it through and in fact, turned my second diagnosis into a win/win.

When delivering my speech I spoke about what many people experience when surviving a life-threatening situation: Changing priorities—not waiting for everything to be perfect to begin to fulfill your life's dreams. I encouraged the audience to make a list of things they want to do "some day" and take baby steps towards those things. I spoke of the curve balls that are tossed our way, the ones that we use as excuses to hold back. I told them about my recent curve ball and pulled off my wig, exposing my bald head to the 1000 member audience. There were gasps in the audience. A standing ovation followed (my first one ever). It was exhilarating!!

• • •

I took a few months off work, but like an idiot, I went back to my job in corporate America. I continued to work for another very stressful year. Finally on June 20, 2005, after 15 years on the job, I walked into my boss' office and told him I couldn't do this anymore. That was my last day.

I walked away from a $100,000 a year job with family health insurance and a pension. My husband was between contracts with no real prospects in site. We had no other health insurance. But this was something I had to do.

My friends thought it was risky but they were very proud of me. My husband was thrilled. He finally had his wife back.

God is Good!! Bill was offered a six week contract job in Alaska the very next day. It was not the one he really wanted, but it got us through. Two months later, he was offered the job that he had been interested in for over three years with the same insurance I had given up. We didn't even have to change providers. He's been there ever since. God is GOOD!!

It is now October 2006. I am working full-time with Sharon at Breast Friends. Breast Friends is growing quickly and we are in the very early stages of developing a formula that would allow us to create affiliates around the country.

We are also developing a national program that would bring cancer support groups into the women's prison system. We've already started the program in Oregon.

I have been blessed with meeting some incredible women as I am traveling all over the country telling my story, hopefully inspiring them to know that God has a plan for all of us. I try to encourage them that when we are thrown a curve ball, we can let it hit us square in the face and knock us down, or we can learn to dodge it. It's a lot less painful. Sharon had the best advice though when I ran all of this past her. She said, "Teach them to do what you did—learn to catch the ball and embrace it." She's right.

I caught the curve ball and used it as a point in my Komen speech with great success. I actually got so excited about the idea of pulling off my wig at the end of my speech, that my husband said, "What if your hair doesn't fall out this time from chemo?"

I replied, "Then I'll have to shave my head."

No problem. It fell out.

• • •

As a two-time breast cancer patient, my odds of surviving appear even a little less encouraging than the first time, but whatever my life expectancy, I will live the time I have with strength, dignity (as much as I can muster), and as much laughter as my heart, and my belly, can handle.

BIBLIOGRAPHY

Wilkinson, B. (2000). Prayer of Jabez. Sisters, OR: Multnomah Publishing, Inc.

Siegal, B.(1988). Love, Medicine and Miracles. New York, NY: Harper & Row.

Radner, G. (1988). It's Always Something. New York, NY: Harper Collins

Rollin, B. (1976). First You Cry. New York, NY: Harper Collins

Biddle, P. (1994). Humor and Healing. Ft. Lauderdale, FL: Desert Ministries

Klein, A.H.H. (1996), Humor in Not-So-Funny Times. Retrieved November 10, 2001 from http://members.aol.com/Usmile2743/humor.notSOfunny.html

Boldt, L. (1999). Zen and the Art of Making a Living. New York, NY: Penguin Putnam, Inc.

Metcalf, CW, Felible, R. (1992). Lighten Up - Survival Skills for People Under Pressure. Cambridge, MA: Perseus Books.